'Quite simply, it is splendid. Future generations will regard *The Norfolk Cranes' Story* as an important contribution to the historical literature of UK bird conservation. John Buxton and Chris Durdin deserve our thanks for telling us the story so well.'

MIKE EVERETT, *BRITISH BIRDS*

'... a heartening and enthralling narrative.'

RICHARD MABEY, *BBC WILDLIFE.*

'... entertainingly relayed ... a definitive account of their story has long been overdue and this book fills the gap admirably.'

TERN, NORFOLK WILDLIFE TRUST.

'The combination of clear readable prose and the relaxed familiarity of the authors with their subject makes the cranes' story interesting for all readers.'

BRITISH TRUST FOR ORNITHOLOGY

Review of *The Norfolk Cranes' Story* by Mike Everett, British Birds, September 2011.

'Having played a small part in the early stages of this story, I have to declare an interest. I worried about being objective here but in the event that was not a problem: this slim volume tells such a straightforward and honest story (and tells it so well) that coming to a fair conclusion about it was easy. Quite simply, it is splendid. It will find a fully deserved place on my shelves alongside those other classics of its genre, George Waterston's *The Return of the Osprey* (1962), John Love's *The Return of the Sea Eagle* (1983) and Roger Lovegrove's *The Kite's Tale* (1990).

'The authors have divided their book into three parts. The second of these covers a range of subject matter, from a brief history of the Common Crane *Grus grus* in the UK to a useful description of the 'Crane country' at and around Horsey (in the Norfolk Broads) and its conservation management to assorted observations on the birds' behaviour. The third part, written by Nick Upton, provides an overview of the status and fortunes of Cranes in Europe, spiced up with a commentary on his efforts to film them.

'It is the first part of the book (more or less the first half, in fact) that I like best. This is John Buxton's account of what happened following the appearance of those first two birds back in 1979. It is very much a personal story, strongly reflecting not just his determination that these new colonists should succeed but also what has become a very deep affection for them. This is good old-fashioned bird protection, and none the worse for that. We are taken through all the highs and lows, the optimism and the disappointment, the disasters and the small triumphs, from the encouraging beginnings of the early 1980s to the 'lean years' of 1989 to 1996 and, finally, on to the much better times that followed.

'Looking back to those early years, I recall that there were some who treated the Horsey story with some cynicism – even ridicule. Their criticisms were unjustified then and seem silly now in the light of what this book tells us. That apart, future generations will regard *The Norfolk Cranes' Story* as an important contribution to the historical literature of UK bird conservation. John Buxton and Chris Durdin deserve our thanks for telling us the story so well.'

The Norfolk Cranes' Story

John Buxton and Chris Durdin

The Norfolk Cranes' Story

John Buxton and Chris Durdin

Chris Durdin

Horsey Estate

FSC
www.fsc.org
MIX
Paper from responsible sources
FSC® C113523

Planting trees to catch carbon
9762847
Printed on Carbon Captured paper

Cover illustration – Cranes over Brograve Mill by Martin Woodcock

Contact
Chris Durdin, 36 Thunder Lane, Norwich NR7 0PX
chris@honeyguide.co.uk

ISBN 978-1-9998386-5-2
First published 2011 by Wren Publishing, 4 Heath Road, Sheringham, Norfolk, NR26 8JH
This paperback edition published in 2019 by Horsey Estate c/o Horsey Hall, Great Yarmouth, NR29 4EF. Design by Nik Taylor.
Additional design by David Abery of Gowise Print (www.gowise.co.uk) for this paperback edition.
Printed in Great Britain by Swallowtail Print (www.swallowtailprint.co.uk) on paper certified by the Forest Stewardship Council (www.fsc.org) as having been produced sustainably.

Contents

Foreword

If you don't know cranes, think of a pair of deer in a spring-time wood: quiet, secretive, watchful, often anxious, needing to be alone in their own space but determined to defend it. So, too, with cranes in an April fen: hidden among reeds, immersed in solitude. The great fens of Britain had solitude...and they had nesting cranes. In winter – like the deer – they became sociable and gregarious; great flocks bugled and trumpeted within the vast tracts of fen as well as over the wide, wild, waterscapes. Then 17th century man took away the fens and the floods and so, too, the cranes.

The next person to see nesting cranes in Britain was John Buxton. They arrived on his patch in Norfolk and because he knew that cranes needed their own private space, he became determined to help them. Without his single-minded efforts to protect the birds and their nesting sites, there would be neither the breeding population nor the wintering flock of cranes that grace the Norfolk Broads today. This is his story: a story of one man's quiet, watchful and often anxious determination to protect the cranes of Horsey. His cranes, their man.

Chris Durdin widens the view. Only by seeing cranes' behaviour can one understand their needs and only by knowing their needs can one try to provide them with conditions suitable for their success: safe sites for nesting and roosting, insect-rich meadows for foraging, summers of solitude. As well as committing John Buxton's story to paper, Chris describes how John has created solitude and other qualities for cranes at Horsey: managing the land and asking for the co-operation of people.

This book is a conclusion to the 30 years' effort by one man in one place; it will surely inspire others to work for cranes in many places. One example is the RSPB's Lakenheath Fen nature reserve in Suffolk. The newly created wetland here includes large, undisturbed areas of reeds with pools and ungrazed fen close by; two pairs have nested since 2007 and first reared a youngster in 2009. Perhaps such features can be incorporated into other large areas of wetland presently being put back into places where wetland used to be. Then many more of these elegant sentinels may emerge from the depths of specially created, wild fens so that we all shall see flights of cranes trumpeting and bugling below Britain's winter skies.

Norman Sills
Site Manager, retired
RSPB Lakenheath Fen nature reserve

Introduction

2011, hardback edition

"Are you writing a book about these many years of adventures and misadventures with the Eurasian cranes? If not, please do."

These words of encouragement were in a letter to John Buxton in May 2002 from George Archibald, who founded the International Crane Foundation in Baraboo, Wisconsin and was its Director until he retired.

This book tells the story of how common cranes – also known as Eurasian cranes but hereafter called cranes – bred at Horsey in Norfolk, and how they were protected and studied there. From a slow start in the Broads, the re-colonisation of this iconic wetland bird is now taking small but steady steps forwards elsewhere in the UK.

Their guardian at Horsey was – and is – John Buxton. Much of what we know about cranes in the UK is contained in John's memory and notebooks. During a month's RSPB sabbatical project in early 2008, Chris Durdin started to capture that knowledge on paper. With John providing the information and Chris doing the writing, this was how the book began and was completed.

This also explains the structure of the book. Part one tells the story of cranes at Horsey in John's words, as told to Chris. Much of this draws on John's memories and the many and detailed notebooks that John kept. Added to these are the diaries, reports and recollections of others, such as Peter Allard, Mike Everett and several crane wardens. The Estate's notebooks are valuable contemporary accounts and are in places quoted almost word for word, with light editing for readability. The same applies to information and quotes from reports of crane wardens, which are woven into John's accounts. Editorial additions to these accounts are indicated by square brackets.

Distances in the notebooks were mainly in imperial measurements (yards and miles), so rather than change these to metric we have kept them as they were originally written. For the most part we have also used imperial measures elsewhere in the book, but we have been relaxed about using metric measurements when that seemed natural, for example using metres to describe the depth of Horsey Mere. Another style point is that we have used lower case species names, contrary to many bird books; we think it is easier on the eye to have cranes rather than Cranes in the middle of sentences.

In some years, it may look as if very little happened, or rather that there is little to tell that sheds useful light on the cranes. This is partly because some nests were in an area that was difficult to access or view, so information on these birds and their breeding activities really is sparse. By contrast, another regular nesting area was much easier to observe. The year by year accounts include elements of the story that are linked to that year, but more general notes on behaviour and related subjects are in part two.

Part two has some context: the history of cranes in the UK, how 'Crane Country' was shaped, and information on land management as it affects crane habitats for breeding and feeding. Observations on their behaviour at Horsey show the time and energy that John Buxton and his team of wardens have dedicated to cranes. The difficulty of access into fens and the birds' secretive and sensitive nature make the observations made at Horsey especially valuable. We hope these will prove useful to land managers elsewhere in the UK as crane numbers increase.

Though this book is primarily about Norfolk's cranes, the common crane is the most widely distributed of the 15 crane species. In part three, Nick Upton describes the challenges facing cranes in the rest of Europe, charting their recent rise in numbers that has contributed to their reappearance in the UK.

The link between John, Chris and cranes goes back a long way. After three years at RSPB headquarters – that famous address of The Lodge, Sandy, Bedfordshire – Chris moved to the RSPB's East Anglia Regional Office, as it was then called, in October 1981. That winter, he was told in confidence about the nesting cranes. With the RSPB Regional Officer, John O'Sullivan, he went to see John Buxton at Horsey in March 1982 to see how the Society could best help that coming season. Chris was included in the team watching over the cranes and, in May that year, did two shifts on protection duties, watching over the nesting site from a small hide.

This first *ad hoc* team quickly became better organised. For the first decade of the cranes' protection, there were usually two wardens throughout the nesting season. The Horsey Estate employed one and the RSPB financed the other, both working under John's supervision. During the 1990s, the amount of wardening effort was much reduced, most of it done by John.

Chris's direct involvement in cranes then slowed, but never stopped. This included taking a steady trickle of calls to the RSPB regional office about cranes from the media, birdwatchers and the general public, giving information designed to keep their presence as a breeding bird low key.

Steadily, as the years went by, the nesting cranes became an open secret and finally public knowl-edge. In recent years, the birds have started to spread away from their core area around Horsey into other parts of the Broads, the Fens and elsewhere while, using crane eggs brought from Germany, a reintroduction project into western England is underway.

So this seems like the ideal time to tell the Norfolk cranes' story; in effect, how it all began. But as they still continue to nest at Horsey and they remain easily disturbed, specific nesting sites within the Horsey Estate and elsewhere are deliberately not described.

2019, second edition

How much interest would there be in a book about the return of cranes to Norfolk? That was the question John Buxton and I faced as we planned the first edition of the book. That we sold out illustrates the appeal of cranes as a bird and the welcome that they have received as a returning breeding bird to the UK, initially in Norfolk and later elsewhere.

The cranes' story at Horsey is strongly linked to John, their guardian there over more than three decades until his death in January 2014. This book stands as a tribute to him. John's years of involvement helped to decide how much to update the book in this second edition: his death is a natural end date for the text. With that in mind, three years are added to the accounts in Chapter 6: we wrote these together at the time. An anecdote about secrecy in the early years came to light after the first edition was published: that is on page 48. John's obituary, as published in the journal British Birds, is included as Appendix 4.

The Horsey Estate is now managed by Robin Buxton, John's son, and Bridget Buxton, John's widow, still lives nearby. Robin, Bridget and I decided to leave everything else, minor tidying of the text aside, as John and I wrote in 2011. A few things change, of course. Crane 'pair D' moved to what we then called 'another river valley'. It is now public knowledge that cranes are in the Ant Valley in or near the RSPB's Sutton Fen nature reserve. Management of the Horsey Estate was then supported and influenced by the Broads Environmentally Sensitive Area (ESA); in 2019 it is in Environmental Stewardship; post-Brexit that mechanism is likely to change again, though the practicalities of management should be similar. Chapter 11 on the future for cranes remains as we saw it in 2011. The main development since is the steady progress of the Great Crane Project, the reintroduction programme based in Somerset. From 93 released birds a breeding population has become well-established, recently spreading to south Wales.

In 2018, there were 54 pairs of cranes in the UK of which 46 pairs attempted to nest, and an estimated population of 186 birds. Roughly half of these are in the introduced population and half in the natural recolonisation that includes the Fens, Yorkshire and Scotland as well as the Norfolk Broads. The cranes' story that started in 1979 looks set to continue.

Chris Durdin, March 2019

Acknowledgements

John's wife Bridget's role in crane protection has been vital. As well as supporting John, she looked after many crane wardens, several of whom stayed at Horsey Hall. She has contributed her own recollections and given great hospitality as we worked in her house.

A team of wardens helped to protect and study the cranes. We apologise if we have missed anyone from these lists. RSPB wardens 1981 to 1990: Rosemary Rodd, Edna Gorney, Sandra Anderson, Minette Bell-MacDonald, Genevieve Leaper, Sandra Worrall, Sally Glass, Jerry Tanguay. Horsey Estate team (mostly contract staff): Robert Gifford, Hilary Marshall *née* Scott, Russell Neave, Samantha Carradice, Nick Peet and John Hampshire.

Norfolk Wildlife Trust staff and volunteers have played a big part in protecting cranes at Hickling and Martham, especially John Blackburn and Richard Starling. John provided information about cranes nesting at Hickling from 2003 onwards. David North from NWT HQ also gave advice. The Trust was known as the Norfolk Naturalists' Trust until 1994, but we usually refer to it by its current name.

Similarly, Robin Lang and Steve Prowse from The National Trust have had a valuable role in local conservation management and crane protection, and Steve has a wider role on the UK Crane Working Group, which he chaired until 2011. Kevin Bull from Natural England contributed information from Yorkshire.

Peter Allard provided his account of the cranes' arrival and other activity in the early years. Christopher Cadbury assisted the Horsey Estate with funding for wardening. Peter Crook provided local information. Julie Durdin and Mary Gamblin proofread drafts. Bill Makins reviewed the account of the captive-rearing experiment. Jo Parmenter helped greatly with the Crane Country chapter. Ralph Todd provided valuable comments and ideas at the draft stage. Daniel Van de Bulk helped with the organisation of many thousands of photographs taken by John over several decades, as well as with wardening and conservation management on the Horsey Estate.

The RSPB provided four weeks' sabbatical time for Chris Durdin that started this project. Ciaran Nelson, then in the RSPB regional office in Norwich, carried on with the media and other public affairs work in Chris's absence, and patiently accepted the diary changes in setting up the sabbatical. Tom Bridge, Joan Childs, Mike Everett, Peter Newbery, Richard Porter, Ian Robinson, John Sharpe, Guy Shorrock, Norman Sills and Andrew Stanbury from, or formerly with, the RSPB, contributed information, memories or comments; Norman also readily agreed to write the book's foreword.

Moss Taylor, as publisher of the first edition and a leading light in Norfolk ornithology over four decades, helped to shape the book in many ways. He also edited an early draft and commissioned Martin Woodcock's superb painting on the cover. The book's design and layout is by Moss's son Nik Taylor.

Nick Upton's chapter on cranes in Europe and his atmospheric photos speak for themselves.

Picture credits
Unless otherwise specified, photographs in this book are by John Buxton and taken at Horsey.

Crane photos on pages 30 and 63, and all photos in part three, Cranes in Europe, are by Nick Upton (except cork oak *dehesa*). The silhouettes on the opening pages to the three chapters are also by Nick Upton, many of whose photographs are on the Nature Picture Library (www.naturepl.com) and RSPB Images (www.rspb-images.com).

Other photographs:
Peter Allard: dead crane at Mundesley p.41.
Chris Durdin: mounted crane in case at Horsey Hall p.65, herb Robert p.102 and cork oak *dehesa* p.123.
Paul Glendell (Natural England): John Buxton, inside back cover.
Mike Page (www.mike-page.co.uk): aerial views of Horsey Mere p.87 and p. 90.
The black and white photograph of Edward North Buxton on p.20 is taken from a larger family photograph at Horsey Hall, photographer unknown, and Anthony Buxton in a punt by John Markham.

The crane artwork below and on the title page was kindly contributed by Mike Langman (www.mikelangman.co.uk).

The Horsey area on the east Norfolk coast.

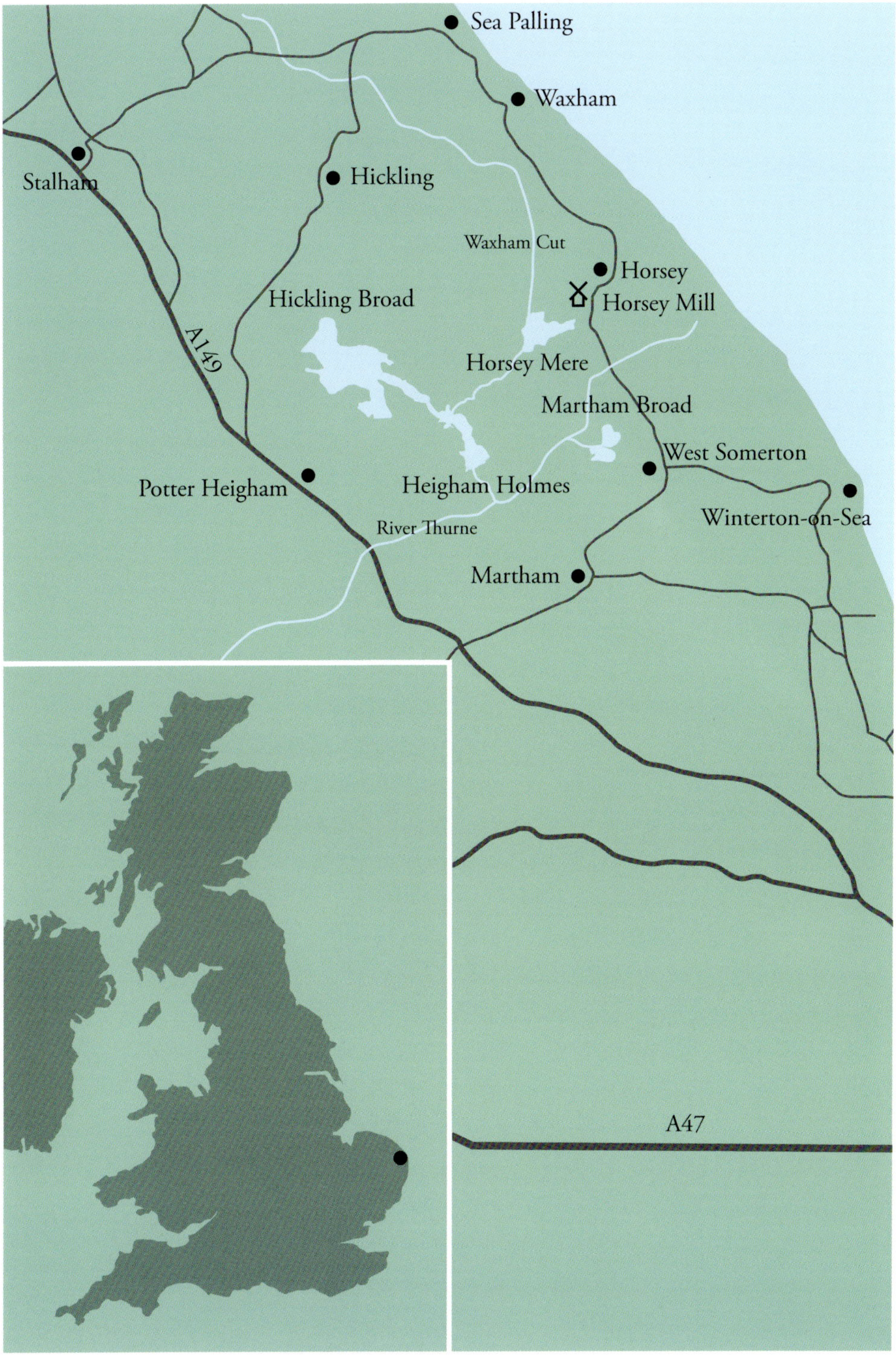

Part One
The Horsey Story

Told by John Buxton to Chris Durdin

Top left: Major Anthony Buxton, John Buxton's father, in the early 1960s. The draw tube telescope, which contributed to the DSO he was awarded, is tucked under his right arm.

Top right: Edward North Buxton, John Buxton's grandfather and founder member of the Fauna and Flora Preservation Society, c. 1896.

Bottom: Major Anthony Buxton in a punt on Waxham Cut, with Jack Russells Hamish, Jane and Ginger, c.1948.

Chapter 1
The Horsey Estate – home of cranes and the Buxton family

It has been an extraordinary privilege to be both witness and guardian of Norfolk's cranes. This book tells their story: how cranes returned to breed in the UK after an absence of 400 years.

The presence of cranes at Horsey in the Norfolk Broads was, at first, a closely guarded secret. When nesting they were, and always will be, sensitive to disturbance, so we avoided publicity for many years. More than 30 years later, their presence here is common knowledge. Cranes have started to expand their breeding range away from Horsey and its neighbouring marshes. Their winter numbers have grown to 50 or more and the winter flock is a regular – if slightly elusive – and popular sight in east Norfolk. So it's a good time both to tell the story of the Norfolk cranes and to put on record some of what I have learned about them while protecting and watching them.

How the Buxton family came to live at the Horsey Estate is entangled with the cranes' story. My father, Anthony Buxton, was a brewer in the family brewery, Messrs Truman, Hanbury, Buxton & Co, in the Spitalfields area of East London. He was commissioned into the Essex Yeomanry Regiment in the First World War, serving in France. Captain Buxton was responsible for a troop of cavalry, later becoming a major in that regiment. Already a keen naturalist, he always carried a draw tube, stalking-style telescope. Curiously, he never used binoculars, then or in later years, always preferring his telescope. He won a Distinguished Service Order (DSO) in unusual circumstances, without firing a gun. In battle, soldiers thought to be the enemy were seen within firing range. He looked with his telescope, saw that they were a troop of the Scots Greys and cancelled the order to fire, thereby saving many lives from 'friendly fire'.

Following the war, which appalled him, he was employed in the Secretariat of the League of Nations in Geneva. By about 1930, I suspect he felt increasingly disappointed at how ineffective the League was proving, and he was certainly looking for a change of direction in life. Though Buckhurst Hill near Epping in Essex was home, he had many relations in Norfolk and he heard that the Horsey Estate was on the market. Lady Lucas was the owner. The estate covered about 1700 acres, some of which was arable farmland but the core of which was Horsey Mere, surrounded by reedbeds. He travelled by train from Geneva with my mother and from Norwich railway station to Horsey by taxi with the agent, Colonel Stewart Horner, to have a look. My mother was from Beauly, near Inverness, and was rather disappointed by the flatness of the countryside around Horsey. My father decided to look round the marshes and was hugely impressed when he saw a pair of marsh harriers flying over the reedbeds. I think he probably made his decision there and then that this is where he wanted to live. He made an offer that was accepted, and that was how the Buxtons came to live at Horsey. I feel I owe the harriers a great debt of gratitude and retain a special allegiance to them.

My father bought the Horsey Estate, including Horsey Hall, in 1930. Initially it was leased for two years to Lady Kennet, mother of the naturalist and painter Peter Scott, who was then at university. After those two years passed, we moved from Geneva. My father and the family arrived in 1932 and immediately set about looking after the birds and the various things that interested him enormously in this wetland site. He employed a keeper-cum-warden, George Crees, who had lived with the family in Geneva, where he was employed to look after a pack of beagles. George also came from Essex and he too had become very keen on the birds and wildlife under my father's guidance.

The first memory I have of Horsey was as a small boy, aged four. I remember the water and the reedbeds, in particular, always fascinated me. My father was hugely enthusiastic about all the birds: bitterns, marsh and Montagu's harriers and bearded tits and other special wildlife. Here my three sisters and I grew up, mucking about in boats on Horsey Mere and the dykes through the adjacent marshes.

My father was very keen on wildlife photography, then black-and-white stills as well as ciné. He had very heavy and complex cameras that I had to carry around. In spring I was sent out, usually in shorts, to wade through the sedge. Saw-sedge cuts like a knife on bare legs, but I don't remember complaining. The aim was to find out where marsh harriers were nesting. My father would be in a hide up a tree directing me with his handkerchief held one way or the other. I usually reached the right place and the excitement of the bird getting up from a nest was a special thrill. This was always after they had hatched, to check how many young were there.

I learned much about the life of marsh harriers. One of the most fascinating facts about this bird of prey is its way of passing food from male to female – the male dropping a prey item such as a small mammal or mallard duckling for the female to catch – and the fascination of watching a 'food pass' from a hide has never left me. I remember one female harrier that was not very good at catching – though she got better – but it seemed to annoy the male when she failed, as he then had to look for the prey she had dropped, and he was often unsuccessful. Poor bird, after all that hard work.

I was in the army for three years from 1946, in the immediate post-war period, stationed mostly in Germany in the British Army of Occupation serving with the Royal Norfolk Regiment. For much of this time I was based in Westphalia, south of Hamburg. I remember watching flights of cranes overhead in the autumn and thought then what marvellous birds they would be to know better. I spent six months in Berlin. This was shortly before the airlift by the Allies to supply Berlin during the Soviet blockade of overland supply routes through what was then East Germany.

I then went to Cambridge to study agriculture for three years, which was followed by a one-year placement on a mostly arable farm near Woodbridge, in east Suffolk, owned by my cousin Giles Foster. Horsey remained my home for holidays, where I was expecting to take over the running of a tenanted farm after my studies were complete. In fact, this farm did not come 'in hand' for the Estate to run until 1984, when the tenant retired.

In 1948, while I was away in the army, my father decided to negotiate a lease to make over the freehold of the Horsey Estate to the National Trust. He was conscious of the challenges in maintaining and protecting what he felt should be an important nature reserve, which the National Trust is able to do in perpetuity through powers granted by an Act of Parliament. The arrangement was that the Buxtons would continue to manage the estate, as before, on a 99-year lease from the National Trust to the family.

From the diaries of Jim Vincent, gamekeeper to Lord Desborough at Hickling Broad and marshes, it was clear that he was much involved with the management at Horsey under its former owner, Lady Lucas. Hickling became a nature reserve of the Norfolk Naturalists' Trust (later re-named the Norfolk Wildlife Trust) some years later in 1945. Jim remained a good friend and adviser to the Horsey team. In 1958, I married Bridget, and took over the leasehold of the Estate. My father continued to live at Horsey Hall with us until his death in 1970. Now, my son Robin holds the lease of the estate. The Horsey Estate Trust looks after the lease of the nature reserve portion of the Horsey Estate, while the National Trust owns the freehold.

Horsey Hall.

The mix of habitats and their location must play a large part in the reason why cranes were attracted to the Horsey area. The east of Britain in general, and Norfolk in particular, have long been known in the bird world for attracting vagrants. The Scandinavian population of nesting cranes moves through continental Europe and into France and Spain in autumn and winter, so the large wetland complex in the Horsey, Hickling and Martham area of the Thurne Broads, adjacent to the coast, is ideally located for the occasional bird to visit on this side of the North Sea.

The Horsey area has two particular attractions to cranes compared with other wetlands near the east coast. Firstly, as well as the wetland mix of open water, reedbed, sedge fen and grazing marsh, there are areas within and adjacent to the Horsey Estate under cultivation. Cranes in winter like to feed in arable fields, for example on the pickings available in maize stubbles in Extremadura in Spain. In the Horsey area they feed on potatoes, either left after harvest or put out for them.

Secondly, Horsey is run as a private estate where there is limited access for the public. The many visitor-friendly nature reserves on or near the east coast, while very valuable for wildlife and people, may be suitable for cranes to visit occasionally or maybe spend part of a winter, but staying to breed is another matter. Nesting cranes are sensitive to disturbance so need large areas well away from people, which has been a key factor in their success at Horsey.

The coastal location of this part of the Norfolk Broads may well have attracted cranes, initially to over-winter and then to breed, but it also brings to mind the area's history and raises a question mark over its long-term future. The River Thurne was once connected to the sea near Horsey; it is not known when the Thurne started to flow southwards towards the River Bure. The connection to the sea was again a reality when this low-lying area flooded with sea water in February 1938, affecting 7469 acres (3024 hectares) including Hickling Broad, Heigham Sound, Martham Broad and Horsey Mere and their surrounding marshes. Sea water again came in from Sea Palling in January 1953, moving along Waxham Cut and into Horsey Mere and killing freshwater fish. Despite seven lives lost at Sea Palling and more elsewhere, the impact on the freshwater marshes was less than in 1938, with about 1200 acres (490 hectares) affected. Though the essentially freshwater nature of the Upper Thurne broads and marshes re-established itself after both of the major floods in the 20th century, a slight saline influence remains. In the light of climate change and relative sea-level rise, the long-term future for sea defences between Sea Palling and Winterton is uncertain, and so too is the length of time that the Horsey-Hickling area will remain as largely freshwater wetlands. I have great faith in the present wall and the engineering expertise with which it was built, but it must be properly maintained. If the sea wall were breached again, salt water would invade Upper Thurne and destroy a unique freshwater habitat.

Peter Scott at Horsey

Sir Peter Scott visited Horsey a few times in later years, including during April 1985, after the cranes had started to nest. On this occasion, a visit with Lady Philippa Scott, he took just five minutes to do this charming line drawing of the 'grey birds', with colour wash added later. Sir Peter was here in the company of the Duke and Duchess of Wellington, Lord Aubrey Buxton and Caroline Keith. The party was requested to crawl along some 50 yards of long grass overlooking the marshes, so they would not disturb the cranes. Sadly, no photographs of the distinguished crawling party were taken. Lady Philippa wrote to me in the autumn of 2009, shortly before she died, recalling how much she and Sir Peter had enjoyed that visit.

Another distinguished guest, HRH Prince Philip the Duke of Edinburgh, visited with Aubrey Buxton on October 1991. His timetable meant he had to rush away and he missed the cranes, seen well on this occasion going to roost. Prince Charles was due to visit on another occasion but had to cancel due to snow. The idea of coming instead by helicopter was mooted, but discouraged to avoid frightening the cranes. So, despite their interest, none of the Royal Family has yet seen the cranes at Horsey. But I did very briefly meet Her Majesty the Queen, indirectly on account of the cranes, when I was presented with an MBE in 2007 "for services to conservation in Norfolk".

Buxton family tree

Sir Edward North Buxton MP
1812 – 1858

Sir Thomas Fowell Buxton GCMC, MP
1837 – 1915

Leland Buxton
1884 – 1967

Major Aubrey Buxton KCVO, MC, Lord Buxton of Alsa
1918 – 2009
Conservationist and founder of Survival Anglia wildlife TV series

Cindy Buxton b.1950
Wildlife film-maker

Edward North Buxton MP
1840 – 1924
Founder member in 1903 of Fauna & Flora International*

Major Anthony Buxton DSO
1882 – 1970
Soldier and writer. Bought Horsey Estate in 1930

John Buxton MBE
1927 – 2014
m. Bridget *née* de Bunsen
b. 1937

9 others

*formerly the Fauna and Flora Preservation Society

Chapter 2
'The biggest bloody herons'
1979 – 1981

1979
Cranes appear at Hickling and Horsey

In September 1979, a tenant farmer who had some cattle grazing in the marshes rang me up with some excitement in his voice to say that he had "Just seen the biggest bloody herons I have ever seen in my life," in fact two of them.

It was Frank Starling, father of Richard Starling, who is now warden for the Norfolk Wildlife Trust's nature reserve at Martham and Starch Grass. I was away in Scotland at the time but from his description I suspected that they might be cranes, and there they were when I returned. I had seen cranes high flying over Horsey in the past, but this was the first time I'd seen any on the ground.

The first appearance of cranes was on 13th September when two birds came to Hickling. They were first seen on the afternoon by Stuart Linsell, then Norfolk Wildlife Trust warden at Hickling Broad, in a stubble field along Stubb Road, Hickling. Local bird recorder Peter Allard saw them on 15th September. A third bird joined them on 10th October, by which time they were moving between Hickling and Horsey. Another tenant farmer, Mr Ernie King, then near retirement, had a field of potatoes that he had not harvested, which the cranes seemed to find delectable. This is where they mostly fed, while roosting in various places in the marshes. I realised then that it was important that they were undisturbed, but I had several hides from which I could watch them without disturbance. Three birds overwintered here, and it later became apparent that they were a pair (hereafter called Pair A) plus a lone individual.

1980
Cranes stay at Horsey, but don't breed

Farmer Michael Kittle had captured a fourth crane at Irstead Hall on 7th October 1979, an exhausted adult. It had either nylon or a rubber object tangled round its bill – I didn't see it myself, and accounts vary. Hilary Scott records that it was kept 'in a wildfowl refuge without restriction until spring 1980', this probably accounting for the fourth bird that joined the original three from 21st March 1980, then present in the Horsey area for at least 11 days to the 31st March.

People said the cranes were bound to leave in the spring, which proved correct. They left Horsey on 5th April, the event witnessed by Terry Boulton from Caister who noted that they circled up very high over Heigham Holmes at 10.50 am, calling frequently as they gained height, circling up to an estimated height of between 2,500 and 3,000 feet. Both Terry and Peter Allard worked for Bristow Helicopters for some 30 years each, so had some experience of estimating height. The cranes then slowly drifted west until they were lost to view, and re-appeared over Sheringham in north Norfolk at midday. Three cranes, presumably these, were seen at Scar House Reservoir, in Upper Nidderdale in Yorkshire on 6th April. They returned two and half weeks later on 22nd April. A later three-day exploratory flight led to sightings over Burton-on-Trent and, on 1st May, over Holyhead in Anglesey. These movements are likely to be an attempted migration back to Scandinavia, but deterred by the hazardous North Sea crossing.

The original group of three cranes, here feeding in a potato field on the Horsey Estate in February 1980.

If nothing else, these movements point strongly towards a wild origin for the three initial birds, contrary to some rumours that the birds were escapees from a collection. These rumours probably reduced interest in the birds' presence, and I didn't discourage this belief. But no information has come to light about cranes escaping from captivity and, by contrast, there are many records of migrants/vagrants in most parts of the UK in all months of the year.

The three cranes were showing clear signs of having become a pair plus a singleton, as these observations, recorded in the Estate's notebook on 30th April 1980, reveal:

> 'At 11 am, I saw them fly in near the Mere, having landed on a reed stubble [left after the reedbed was cut]. The larger male and female were together and the single, smaller male rather left out on his own. Their behaviour is more and more paired off plus one.'

Peter Allard's notes confirm that the cranes returned on 22nd April 1980, then on the potato fields at Horsey, and that two quickly paired up, leaving the third bird by itself. Peter's notes recall:

> 'This single bird stayed in the fields until 7th May while the pair was exploring more reedy areas. There were four cranes present again on May 18th, the third bird having re-appeared on the 14th being joined by a fourth on the 18th. These additional birds were not seen again after this date or throughout the summer, but the [original] pair remained very secretive in the reedbeds and was rarely seen. I saw them displaying and throwing mud clumps around on several occasions.'

The bustle is raised when a crane is excited.

This third, single bird, which was not part of the pair, was recognisable by its pale 'bustle'. I describe the bustle as the feathers that look like a tail when the wings are folded, though in fact they are not tail fathers, rather the elongated inner secondaries of the wings held at the back of the bird.

The bustle is quite an expressive signal of the birds' mood. It is normally held low, but is raised when they are courting or if alarmed, for example by a fox. When suspicious, a crane will stretch upright with the neck extended, with the bustle slightly raised.

The male of Horsey's first pair of cranes had a black bustle and the female a grey bustle lightly streaked with black. This is not a difference between the sexes as there is continuous variation in a crane population in the shade of the bustle, from black to grey. It is pure chance that the male of this pair had one extreme and the female the other. The difference in bustle colour is not apparent in flight. The male is slightly larger than the female and this is a sexual difference.

It was becoming clear that the third bird was a male due to the extent of red on his head and low-key antagonism between the two male birds, raising the wings and calling. The pair and the lone male became more physically separated, as stated in the Estate notebook dated 8th May 1980:

> 'One crane seen at 8 am flying over the Mere. 10 am two cranes both with black tail coverts [meaning the bustle] were seen back on the usual feeding place on sown barley. No sign of the pale-tailed one. Much less sign of them courting now and despite reports to the contrary they don't seem to be itching to nest, I am afraid. Anyway, it is good to have them back.'

With hindsight, I realise it was already a little late to start nesting. Later, a pattern emerged of the first egg being laid during the second half of April – three pairs laying in the first week of April 1995 being a notable exception – though later re-laying also happened several times after first clutches were lost.

I observed them pretty closely in the spring and summer of 1980 and was worried that bird-watchers might see them, but happily they were in an area where they couldn't readily be seen. They appeared to be showing territorial behaviour, but didn't nest. This behaviour included flapping their wings, dancing and calling in unison, but without choosing a nest site. Subsequently, I deduced that they were immature, two or three years old, as opposed to four or five, which is the normal age at first breeding. No other cranes were decoyed down by the calling birds. They remained throughout the autumn and into the next winter, feeding on potatoes left out for them.

We had tried to keep to a minimum the number of people who knew about the cranes, but how secret were they really? Peter Allard, Don Dorling and Michael Seago, key members of the Norfolk bird recording team for many years, knew about them. Ted Ellis, the much-loved

Norfolk naturalist, who lived in the Broads, wrote a daily nature column in the Eastern Daily Press under his initials E.A.E., and had a hand in making them more widely known. Peter takes up the story.

> 'The news of these cranes wintering in east Norfolk 1979-80 was a very closely guarded secret and only known to John Buxton and Stuart Linsell, the locals and a very few birdwatchers, namely myself, Michael Seago and Don Dorling. On February 28th 1980, Ted Ellis, having heard word of the cranes at Horsey, published in his *Eastern Daily Press* column an article entitled 'Twitchers Beware', which mentioned the cranes wintering in east Norfolk and gave a few clues as to where they were. The secret was out within a few days as a local Norwich birdwatcher had quickly found their roosting and feeding areas almost the following day. The Norfolk birders' grapevine was very busy that weekend much to the annoyance of myself, Michael and obviously John Buxton.'

So even at this early stage there were birders who knew that cranes had spent the spring and summer at Horsey, and inevitably that number would grow. Similarly, they were known about locally, though whether word spread is not clear. Peter Crook, a birdwatcher living in Hickling village, saw a crane on Brograve Levels in June 1981, and saw them displaying at around that time. He recalls at least four other locals, mostly those who worked on the marshes, who knew about their year-round presence.

1981
First nesting attempt: two eggs laid, one chick hatched but lost to an unknown predator.

In April 1981, Pair A began nest building in a marsh area of almost pure saw-sedge, *Cladium mariscus*. Two preliminary nest platforms were built in about 18 inches of water among saw-sedge that had been harvested the year before. The next nest was built on the edge of a thicker, mature clump of saw-sedge with an open area of a few yards' extent around the clump. These three stages of nests were built over a ten-day period. The last of the three became the final nest and was, by good luck, within 200 yards of an observation hide that had been in place for some years.

The subsequent nesting activity was observed from this distance from a slightly elevated point eight feet above ground level. This view allowed sight of an adult crane on the nest, when its head was up, but one could not see onto the nest surface due to obstructing vegetation. Nest building lasted only three days at this final site and there was much carrying and walking to and fro by both birds. The female spent more time on the nest adjusting and stepping about to build the platform to her satisfaction, while the male placed small pieces of vegetation at her disposal. The nest material was gathered by walking around within a few yards of the site.

The water regime of the nest site marsh is that it has drainage dykes (ditches are known as dykes in the Norfolk Broads) surrounding it, with water levels varying according to the main river levels. In winter, the water on the marsh may be up to 2½ - 3 feet deep. In the normally lower summer levels, the marsh may dry up altogether; the cranes choose a site where the water level at nest-building time is about 18 inches deep around the nest platform.

A consistent point is that the male and female are not seen feeding together away from the nest during the incubation period. From the time of the first egg being laid the male or female would fly off, on their own, to feed at their favoured grass marsh area. In the case of the female this was up to half a mile distant and the male up to a mile away. Incubation time was shared fairly evenly, with the female spending slightly longer periods on the nest. Incubation at night was always by the female when the male would roost close by, standing on one leg in the water. In the first week or so, the cranes' unison call was given at changeover between the male and female, but this stopped after about a week.

Judging by whether cranes were being seen singly or two together, the first eggs were lost on 22nd April, probably due to flooding. They appeared to be incubating again by 6th May.

The RSPB was told about the cranes at an early stage and Mike Everett, species protection officer, visited to advise. Mike kept a journal and here takes up the story.

> '12th May 1981 … a summons from John Buxton, with good news from Horsey, sent me scampering up there this morning. John O'Sullivan had beaten me to it by perhaps half a minute when I arrived there at 10.30. The good news, of course, is that the cranes have made a definite nesting attempt, at last...
>
> 'We had a general discussion first, during which I agreed to find and finance an additional warden for a month, to start as soon as possible. Then we went in the Landrover to the private side of the reserve where, very sensibly, the cranes have chosen to nest. From a makeshift but quite splendid hide (from which the actual nest is not visible) we had stupendous views of the male, who was busily feeding only 120 yards away; the female was presumably on the nest. He was totally unconcerned by us, it seemed, but we became quite concerned when, after a little while, he flew towards us and commenced feeding not 50 yards away! Since we were anxious not to upset him in any way, we felt we could not leave the hide while he was so close to it. In effect, we were marooned inside! We now had even more amazing views of this handsome and stately bird, especially with our telescopes. We could clearly make out the extent of the small fringe of red colouring around the base of the bill, and even distinguish what seemed to be a bare, red triangular patch on the underside at the base.
>
> 'His walk was the ultimate in deliberate elegance; when feeding, his body was held horizontal (prompting JOS [John O'Sullivan] to remark that his legs seemed to be set much too far forward) and his head was held well down near the ground. On alert, he looked a totally different bird, standing tall and very upright. He fed (or, at least, probed) almost continuously with a short, downwards-stabbing movement of his bill, but although we clearly saw him swallowing many times we could not see what he was actually eating. From time to time, judging by his lifted head and bill movements, he seemed to call quietly, presumably to his sitting mate – but due to the strong wind we could not actually hear him.
>
> 'Finally, we did manage to escape from the hide, without alarming the crane too much.'

The two birds were again seen together on 14th May, suggesting that a predator had taken the eggs, then incubating again by 30th May, or perhaps that had started a few days earlier, for a typical incubation period of 30 days. On 23rd June, there was a distinct change in pattern, with the adult cranes no longer tied to the nest. This suggested an egg had hatched. Instead of one adult being away from the nest, both would move from the nest together. Though no chick could be seen, it was plain from the parents' behaviour that they were looking carefully after something as they walked about among the sedge clumps near the nest. Often one adult would go off to feed on the grazing marshes, leaving the other moving around close to the nest, attending to the young bird. Both adults would still come back to the nest overnight.

Pair A – the first cranes to nest in the UK for some 400 years.

The estate had taken on Hilary Scott to help with wardening duties. Three weeks after hatching she heard a high peeping sound, which was plainly a chick. The adult pair walked close to the hide, but the chick, by then probably about six inches tall, could not be seen in the thick cover.

Around this time, water levels started to rise in the marsh and I was concerned about the nest on which the family of cranes was roosting overnight. While they were away, I went to the nest, moved it to one side, built up the platform with more vegetation, made it solid by squashing it down and returned the nest to the higher level. The birds returned and climbed onto the now higher pile without hesitation.

The chick ranged farther and farther out from the nest, always accompanied by one or both parents, and reached the stage of walking out to the adjacent grazing marshes at three weeks of age. Then, about a week later, the adult pair could be seen feeding together again on the grazing marshes, very clearly with no chick. It is likely that the chick at this stage was lost to a predator, perhaps a fox, out on the open marsh.

We don't know what happened to the second egg. I suspect that a marsh harrier ate it while on the nest – they are known to take moorhen and other birds' eggs – but this is speculation. Though bitterns are potential predators I did not suspect them as their nest was about half a mile away. Then, foxes were less likely suspects as predators in the fen. Now they have easy access through the thick sedge and reed following the paths made by Chinese water deer, but the deer at that time had not arrived at Horsey, so access for foxes was more difficult.

So, in 1981, for the first time in several centuries, a crane had hatched in the UK. But we would have to wait another year for the more important milestone of the first chick to be fledged.

Chapter 3
Early years – the first chicks fledge, but progress is slow 1982 – 1988

1982

Pair A nested in the same place and for the first time fledged one young, which was later found to be a male.

These two cranes spent the winter in the Horsey area and were again fed with potatoes. They took up an obvious territory, with the nest site within 30 yards of the 1981 site.

Mike Everett was keen to mark the eggs because of the risk from egg collectors. Marks with invisible ink mean that forensic tests can identify the eggs should they be stolen. The RSPB had been marking the eggs of raptors and other birds for several seasons and, from this experience, Mike was optimistic that the cranes would return rapidly to the nest after the marking had been done. I was concerned about the impact of disturbance but eventually I somewhat reluctantly agreed, so long as this task could be done when the male was on the nest. The male and female were spending roughly equal amounts of time incubating, but I judged that going into the nest when the male was there would cause less stress.

Mike Everett (MJE) again takes up the story in his journal of 23rd April 1982.

> 'We went by boat up to [the nest area] and walked in along a side cut to the hide which overlooked the breeding area. Suddenly, we came upon the female crane feeding in an area of cut sedge; not wishing to disturb her, we backtracked and went in by boat instead. But this ploy failed – she saw us and lifted off and flew away. John concluded that (or maybe hoped that) the male was 'on'. We reached the hide and after a quick look decided all was well. At 12.50, John and I set off and walked out into the marsh via a convenient sedge-cutter's path.
>
> 'John had the site pinpointed so well that we found the nest within ten minutes of leaving the hide. The male crane came off at 25 yards and flew away, low and direct, quietly calling 'glogogogogo...' As the photographs opposite show [I had sent photos to Mike] the nest was in a small wet clearing, built mainly of sedges etc. and standing about 12" high but with the bottom 7" in water; it measured roughly 36" x 40". The two curiously elongated eggs lay almost side by side, pointing the same way. At 13.00 precisely, on St George's Day 1982, I became the first man to mark the eggs of *Grus grus* in England, marking both 'GG82' with a Volumatic Security Marker. We could now see both cranes flying together,

silently, in the distance. John had fired off a number of photographs while I was busy with the eggs. We left swiftly and were back in the hide with Hilary by 13.10, having completed the entire operation in 20 minutes. There was now no sign of the birds: Hilary told us they had gone down away to the southeast.'

Mike Everett marked the eggs with invisible ink.

Part of the deal with Mike was that he would stay and watch from the hide to check that they returned, which they did, but it took two hours. Mike again records:

'At 13.15 John and Hilary left me on watch and went back to the mill. I settled down to await events and keep a formal log ...

13.32: Both cranes appear from west - fly past well beyond nest area towards east, calling quietly, and disappear to east as if landing in fields near the Mere. Appreciable size difference - the male presumably the larger.

14.00: Marsh harrier up, very distant. By now I start to worry at the cranes' non-return.

14.13: The cranes plane in and land near the short (cut) sedge area 100 yards to my left ...

14.15: ... but I can't see either of them [due to the thick cover of sedge].

14.20 – 14.30: Both appear well to right of where landed – one walking steadily towards nest area (?? male) – keep losing him in tall vegetation – finally lose him altogether – but he has by 14.30 walked in to the nest. No sign of the other bird either.

14.37: Find head in sedge [with telescope] - looks as if sitting – where I know nest to be.

14.45: By now have bird in 'scope - it is definitely a sitting crane! What relief ... the sex uncertain. Other bird not relocated. *Ergo* was off nest – or nest was left – for one and a half hours, give or take a few minutes.

15.15: All quiet – MJE leaves hide.'

Mike then rowed back to somewhere near the mill, at which point I arrived with Chris Durdin. Mike was able to show us a merlin sitting out on the old windmill.

I was worried by the time that the cranes spent away from the nest after the eggs were marked and vowed not to do this again. While the cranes were away, a male marsh harrier landed in the area of the cranes' nest for a short time, though it wasn't possible to see what it was doing. The harriers' own nest with eggs was roughly 150 yards away.

Looking back nearly 28 years later, Mike still remembers his profound relief that all went well – and that I had to satisfy myself that Mike's conclusions were correct before I was able to relax. In retrospect, Mike agrees that we probably sailed rather too close to the wind on that April day in 1982; he fully agreed with my decision not to mark the eggs in subsequent seasons.

So, happily, incubation was resumed. This season, the hatched chick was seen regularly after the three-week stage when it was being taken on a daily walk to feed on open grazing marshes. This is a regular pattern: up to about three weeks after hatching, the chick will be walked about and fed within the sedge or reed marsh area.

Late evening ... I saw three cranes fly in.

I remember an exciting day, when watching from the hide late one evening about ten weeks after the young crane had hatched. I was expecting the crane family group to walk back to the nest to roost, as had been their usual habit. Suddenly I saw three cranes fly in from half a mile away and alight near the nest. The adults gave a full-throated unison call while the young bird walked onto the nest and stood up looking quite proud of himself. He might well be – he was the first young crane to do so here for some 400 years. Later we discovered this chick was a male, and he became part of a key pair of Broadland cranes for producing young.

The crane family was not alone at Horsey. A third adult was suspected from 5th May and confirmed from 13th May to at least the end of February 1983.

1983

Pair A nested in the same place and, at their second attempt, again fledged one young, later found to be a female.

The nucleus of the family unit from 1982 broke down immediately prior to this year's nesting season. The male chick raised last year was no longer tolerated close to Pair A and took on a solitary, wide-ranging existence. A recognisable hierarchy was established, the male parent being most dominant and actively chasing and displacing the offspring from roosting or feeding sites. The offspring in turn was observed displacing the female and pursuing her to the nest, though aggression between the female and offspring was generally less and the two were occasionally seen feeding together. Prolonged unison calling, in response to the presence of the offspring near the nest, occurred only when the male was incubating or near the nest; when only the female was present there was no reaction. Aggression decreased after the first nest failed and the birds were occasionally seen feeding together. A degree of tolerance was also re-established after fledging and the four cranes were observed in flight together.

The site of both nests was again within an extensive area of saw-sedge marsh, free from disturbance. The nest was made of layers of dry sedge and reeds piled to a height of approximately 18 inches, measuring some 2 – 3 feet in diameter and situated in a cleared area of shallow water 30 feet by 15 feet, eaten out by coypus within the dense marsh several years earlier. Similar smaller open areas within the marsh provided accessible feeding areas from the nest.

Incubation of the first clutch stopped after 13 days. Fox predation was the likely cause of failure. As the nest was under observation, marsh harriers, carrion crows or other aerial predators would probably have been seen. No trace of shell remained near the nest, suggesting a predator large enough to carry off the egg.

The second nest was successful. On hatching and for eight days following, the cranes remained largely in the nesting marsh with the chick, one or other parent flying out occasionally to feed, especially in the evening. From this time until fledging the parents flew only rarely, walking everywhere close to the chick. On the ninth day after hatching, the cranes were sighted for the first time away from the nest, feeding in an area of rough ground, an old flight pond, on the opposite side of the dyke wall bounding the nesting marsh. For the following 12 days they mostly fed here, making occasional forays into neighbouring hayfields, then back in the sedge marsh during the early morning and again roosting in the evening.

The male generally led the movement through a field, seeking appropriate dyke crossing points and remaining alert to danger. The female and chick followed together. The male usually crossed dykes with a short flight, while the female either followed similarly and waited for the chick on the opposite bank or accompanied the chick in climbing down into the dyke and swimming over.

Haymaking prompted the cranes to move onto a wheat field, feeding on the heads by stripping the stalks in an upward movement, though still returning on foot to the nest to roost. During the fortnight prior to fledging, they ranged out into grazing marshes to feed during the day, returning after fledging too.

On its 39th day, the chick showed its first inclinations towards flying, copying its parents by extending and flapping its wings. From the 69th day, the chick fed independently between the parents, though still accepting food on occasions. It fledged successfully on the 74th day after hatching.

Keeping the cranes secret: stallions, mares and foals

Security was always high in our minds. We were anxious to keep word of cranes nesting off the birdwatching grapevine so that the birds should not be disturbed. Egg collecting, then as now, was a fear, and reinforced the need to keep the cranes' presence a secret. As soon as we were confident that the cranes were nesting, an intensive watch was kept from a makeshift but effective hide in a sallow bush about 200 yards from the nest. Handover from one watch to the next was far from straightforward as, to get to the hide, it involved taking the next volunteer over a 'cut', part of the River Thurne but also a major man-made drainage channel.

This was long before mobile phones so communication was a challenge. Using walkie-talkies, we were a little anxious that someone else might find our frequency and hear what was said. So cranes were not mentioned, and the scientific name for cranes *Grus grus* prompted GG or 'gee gee'. The horse code was simple enough: the male crane was the stallion, the female was the mare and the chick was a foal.

Birdwatchers used the public footpath from Horsey Mill to watch roosting harriers and other raptors – this was before the watch point at Stubb Mill, Hickling became established. It worried me that this would bring people in to where the cranes were coming and going. They were kept strictly to the paths and we put up a sign to discourage crowds, but the birdwatching public was not a problem at this stage as the raptor roost was gone by the time cranes were beginning to nest in late March. Security was helped by the large waterway between the footpath and the area where the cranes nested.

The way information spreads was illustrated by a question posed at a conference on cranes in spring 1983. George Archibald, of the International Crane Foundation based at Baraboo, Wisconsin in the USA had met Christopher Cadbury, who was much involved with the Norfolk Wildlife Trust, especially at Hickling. George said he was sure that cranes must be nesting somewhere in the UK and Christopher said that yes, in fact they were, and put George in contact with me. George asked me to attend a conference in Bharatpur, India as the UK representative. Christopher Cadbury kindly financed the trip from a family conservation fund and I attended, along with my wife Bridget, my sister and my brother-in-law. There I was lucky enough to see three Siberian white cranes, one of which was a yellow juvenile, plus many sarus cranes on arable fields in the area.

In my talk about cranes in the UK I refused to say they had bred, though George was aware of the fact. In questions, a representative from East Germany said he had heard that they had nested in Norfolk but that a fox had eaten the chick. I could see George and my family wondering how I would deal with the question. I thanked him for the question and said, "There are always rumours." He was right, of course, but I left it at that, without admitting that the rumour was true. It was an illustration of how effective the bush telegraph can be, even reaching behind the iron curtain, as it was then.

Horsey Mill, February 2008.

The Horsey Estate has always managed the protection of the cranes in house. The RSPB was a great help, especially during the first few years, albeit slightly at arms' length. The Society funded additional seasonal wardens for 10 years and assisted with finding some of the wardens taken on by the Horsey Estate. I was conscious of the risks of publicity, so didn't wish the RSPB to manage the cranes' protection directly. The RSPB was at ease about this, recognising the value of secrecy to protect the cranes and that the partnership was an effective way of managing the project and sharing costs. I was keen to keep the cranes' presence as quiet as possible, in which I was helped by careful handling of enquiries from media and the public at the RSPB regional office, largely dealt with by Chris Durdin as the Society's spokesman.

1984

Pair A plus their two offspring remained all year, and there were two unsuccessful nesting attempts by the adults.

The four cranes split up into two and two from 26th March. The younger two birds then began to wander, on the Norfolk coast and elsewhere in Broadland especially, a pattern that has continued to this day. Peter Allard saw them over his Cobholm (Great Yarmouth) garden at 11 am on 3rd April, circling high at more than 2,000 feet. The adults were rarely seen after the end of March, but joined the two younger birds again from 23rd May after two nest failures. All four remained in the Horsey area until the year-end.

Birdwatcher Bob Cobbold found a dead, adult crane on the tide line at Mundesley on 7th April and Peter Allard photographed it in his back garden on 11th April. Peter phoned me about this bird and, as there were four cranes at Horsey in both 1984 and 1985, we agreed it must have been a migrant and not one of the Horsey individuals. However, it was an interesting occurrence: cranes were still quite a rarity in Norfolk in 1984.

Dead crane found on Mundesley beach, April 1984.

1985

As in 1984, Pair A had two unsuccessful nesting attempts.

The four birds left on 6th January with the onset of blizzard conditions. Presumably, these birds were those seen in Essex and Kent a few days later. They spent several weeks, from January 10th, in fields at Chislet, south of Herne Bay in northeast Kent.

The RSPB warden this year was Minette MacDonald who followed events carefully at the nest site in the usual remote and unmanaged area of marsh. The first egg was laid on 17th April; incubation lasted for 31 days, with both sexes incubating for spells of two to four hours. While changeovers at the nest could be followed, these were often not immediate: sometimes 30 minutes would elapse before the feeding bird would leave the nest site. The female was easy to recognise as she continually painted her upper body and wing coverts a pale brown colour with mud and decaying vegetation from the surrounding area, presumably to be less conspicuous on the nest, whereas the male retained his slate grey colouring. She normally fed fairly close to the nest, whereas the male would go farther afield; he would also chase away the two young cranes if he felt they were too near to the nest.

On 17th May, the day before we thought the egg was due to hatch, the male was in a meadow apparently in a slight state of unrest, pacing about rather than feeding. The female flew from the nest site to join him, the first time since incubation started that both birds were away from the nest. The male approached the female, with wings outstretched and bustle raised; five unison calls were given and they both then returned to the nest. Very shortly after, both birds left the nest for a final time, flying towards the dunes. On entering the nest area soon after I found the chick, drowned a few feet from the nest. Its right leg was deformed and, judging by its size, it had hatched about two days earlier.

On 26th May, the two birds started a second nest, exactly eight days after the death of the chick. The cranes' behaviour followed the same pattern as for the first incubation. Then the birds became more and more inconsistent with their feeding times. The female became quite agitated and spent five to ten minutes, occasionally up to 30 minutes, away from the nest. The male was by then feeding well away and seemed uninterested in the proceedings. On checking the nest on 28th June, a bright orange crane chick swam strongly across the water into the cover of reeds; the chick looked as if it was about two days old.

For the next three days, the adults were observed moving about in the reedbed close to the nest area. Often only their heads were visible as they fed the chick. On 1st July, the three birds had moved onto grazing marshes. Evidently the chick, small though it was, had managed to cross two large dykes. The family party fed there for the next two weeks. On 15th July, several 'krook' calls were heard. Both birds were seen searching for the missing young, flying to and from the nest area, and covering every square inch of their feeding area by walking and bending their heads to look into the long grass. After almost three hours, both adults flew to the far side of Stubb Mill, still calling, returning after ten minutes, then flying off. On two recent days we had seen a fox not far from the cranes' feeding area, and presumably it had taken the crane chick that disappeared. Six hours after the chick was taken, the two adults continued their search, flying backwards and forwards to their feeding area, both giving loud single calls. For two days the birds remained here; on the third day they flew away from the area for the last time.

All four birds remained at Horsey to the end of the year, being joined by a new juvenile bird in November, presumably a migrant. The two offspring of the original pair themselves paired up (hereafter called Pair B).

1986

Pair A made one nesting attempt, successfully rearing a chick.

At the beginning of April, when wardening started, all five cranes were still moving around as a flock and roosting together. From 6th April, Pair A began to be seen apart from the others but were still roosting with them as a group until 16th April.

From the time nest building started, the other cranes were no longer tolerated and were 'seen off' by the male when flying near the nest area. He would fly up behind them, on occasion with a very deliberate, stiff-winged flight, flicking the wing tips at the end of each downbeat.

The other cranes made several attempts at migrating between 13th April and 30th April, possibly in response to the aggression from the male of Pair A. This included three flying out to sea near Horsey Gap on 30th April: they were later seen at Cley, Blakeney and Salthouse on the north

Norfolk coast, returning to Horsey three hours later. Sometimes all three circled up, at other times only two, but they always returned within a few days. The immature bird finally left the area in early May, presumably pushed away during the breeding season by the nesting birds.

For Pair A, by 19th April nest building was definitely in progress in the same area as in previous years. The nest, the usual rough platform of sedge and reed stems, was in a saw-sedge marsh that had been cut the previous summer. Incubation was underway by 24th April, though one or more eggs may have been laid up to three days before that, with incubation lasting 28 days until 21st May. A chick hatched on 22nd May, the date determined from when the adults both walked away from the nest together. Until the tenth day, the family was still roosting at the nest but after that was not seen or heard in the nest area. It seems likely that an old nest site farther south was used as a roost once the family of cranes had moved out onto the open fields to feed.

Sunset over the main flood at Horsey.

On 2nd June, the twelfth day after hatching, repeated alarm calls from 7 to 7.30 am indicated that something was wrong, particularly when both adults flew up together. However, the parents did return, as by 10 am the family of three was feeding on grazing marshes, out of the saw-sedge marsh. It seems possible that both eggs hatched and it was the death of a second chick that disturbed the cranes into temporarily deserting the first chick. The young crane was first seen to fly on 4th August, the seventy-fifth day after hatching.

1987

Pair A made five unsuccessful nesting attempts, and a man-made nest.

The group of cranes now numbered six, including the young bird raised last year. They left Horsey on 12th January following heavy snow, though were reported locally in early February. Three returned on 7th March – I saw two at Horsey on 9th March on the day I returned from Kenya – and the other three on 11th March. There were fairly typical crane records in north Norfolk in late March and early April, then again in mid-May.

A pair of cranes spent the summer moving around various locations in Essex, between 27th May and 20th September. They were mostly by the coast, from Foulness and Potton Island in south-east Essex to Fingringhoe on the Colne Estuary towards the north-east of the county, but also appeared inland at Hanningfield Reservoir where they were seen displaying on the evening of 12th June.

We didn't know about the pair in Essex at the time, and later wondered if they were Pair B, exploring away from home before returning to breed successfully at Horsey for the first time the following year. Three cranes had been seen over Stodmarsh in Kent on 10th March, the day before they reappeared at Horsey on 11th March, raising the possibility that two birds went south again for the summer. Though ringing crane chicks could have helped to identify our birds when away from Horsey, our birds were not ringed, a decision we took to avoid disturbance at the nest. But looking back in our diaries, Pair B was seen at Horsey on several dates in June, so that neat explanation of the Essex birds does not fit: they must have been an additional pair. It is more likely that two cranes reported elsewhere in Norfolk, from Rollesby on 16th June and Worstead on 17th June, were our Pair B, as they were not recorded at Horsey on those dates.

There was no Horsey Estate warden this year, so 24-hour watches of the nest area were impossible. Sandra Worrall stayed between early April and the end of June, when the emphasis of wardening was on preventing disturbance by people. The following notes, about the first four of Pair A's remarkable five nesting attempts, partly summarise and partly quote Sandra's notes taken at the time.

> 'Nest 1: two cranes were seen building a nest on 13th April. When the nest was checked on 20th April, with both birds away, there was no egg.'
>
> 'Nest 2: 25th April, the pair now established at a different site. 1st May: much noise of alarm calls from nest site. Three marsh harriers were over flying it and swooping low. Two cranes flew away. Nest checked: no sign of an egg, with water level up to the cup. Possible explanation: water levels forced the sitting crane off, with the egg subsequently taken by a harrier. 2nd May: Male and female flew in and inspected the nest site before flying off together.'
>
> 'Nest 3: the birds then moved elsewhere on the Estate. The nest site was impossible to observe, but subsequently (21st June) fragments of a crane egg and internal membrane were found there.'

'On 11th May, from 11 am all four cranes were feeding in the fields. At 11.20, the two males flew low, striking each other with their feet and grabbing with their bills. The two younger birds finally flew off in the direction of Somerton at 11.30. At 11.35, a crane of unknown origin flew in. Unlike the usual four, it had begun moulting its flight feathers. All five were at [the nesting area] at c. 4 pm. At c. 6.15 pm, the two older birds mated.'

'Nest 4: 17th May, incubation presumed to have started at a fourth site. 25th May, a birdwatcher who regularly comes to Horsey reported that about an hour earlier he had heard the cranes calling for about ten minutes. Between 8 am and 9 am, John Buxton saw a bittern fly in from its normal territory direct to the cranes' site. It was not challenged and no crane was seen or heard. Bitterns will rob harrier nests and would presumably rob cranes' nests too. 11.30 am: our fears were realised when two cranes were seen flying out of the area. 26th May: JB and I went to the nest area, could not find the actual nest, but there were tracks in the reeds where the cranes had been pushing their way through.'

"Not another hide, surely! Can't they decide where to go..." Cartoon on Sandra Worrall's 1987 wardening report cover.

This pattern of failure prompted me to build a nest where it could be seen, the first attempt to directly help the cranes since the nest platform had been made higher in 1981. The site was a reed pond – an island of reed surrounded by water two feet deep, the whole site extending to about half an acre and overlooked by a hide. Cranes had regularly been feeding and roosting overnight here, but had never nested. A pattern of 'Where I sleeps, I nests' suggested they could be persuaded to nest here. Reed cutting at Horsey finishes by mid-March in most areas so there is no danger of disturbing bitterns, marsh harriers and cranes, all reedbed-nesting birds that plan nest sites in advance of nesting. There is some reed litter left behind after harvest, and a nest platform was constructed using litter from a nearby clearing. The platform, built over reed growing in water two or three inches deep, was roughly three feet in diameter and six inches above the water level, once well-trodden down. On this was added finer material, grass and soft rush, copying what is on a crane's nest. The location chosen was on the edge of the water, giving a view from the platform for cranes, should they decide to use it, and some protection from ground predators by being on an island. It was facing the hide so that any activity could be seen.

It worked, drawing in the cranes to nest again, on their fifth site this year and probably their fourth clutch of eggs, though again without further success. On 11th June, two cranes were together in the reed marsh pond, the female occupying the artificial nest, the male driving away the ducks. Incubation apparently had started. However, there were soon discouraging signs when, on 16th June, the two cranes were feeding together. They continued to sit, but the male took his parental duties increasingly lightly: he would stand near the nest rather than sit on it, and in rain would retreat into the surrounding reedbed, leaving the nest area for up to two hours. And so this final attempt was abandoned.

Measured just by the lack of fledging cranes, the year was a failure, but Sandra Worrall summed up aptly the five breeding attempts this year:

> 'What is remarkable is the sheer tenacity of the adult birds in continuing to attempt breeding against apparently insuperable odds!'

1988

Pair A nested but failed. Pair B nested successfully for the first time and produced one young towards the southern end of the Horsey Estate.

The risk from egg collectors was highlighted by an incident in early May. I was out at the time but a resident of Martham, Harry Cropper, was helping as a volunteer warden. Harry saw a car parked in what he regarded as suspicious circumstances and asked two men coming out of a private hide if they were there with permission. "No, just looking, not doing any harm" was the gist of the reply. Taking the initiative, Harry asked them to leave and escorted them back to the road.

I alerted Stalham police and spoke to Peter Robinson, RSPB Investigations Officer, who visited Horsey with his wife Sue a few days later. According to Peter, the car was in the process of changing ownership but was registered in Yorkshire and belonged to an egg-collector who had been caught in Scotland and Wales during the previous month. On the following day, RSPB warden Sally Glass's car was broken into while it was parked at Horsey Mill and, although probably unconnected, increased the feelings of concern, though no more came of the incident.

Having failed five times last year, it was disappointing to see the original pair of cranes fail again. But Pair B was making much better progress. On 23rd May, a young crane was seen, at 18 or 19 days old already getting bigger and browner instead of the gold of a tiny chick. On 28th May, it was seen again with its parents, which took it in turns to go away to feed, or stay with the chick.

Pair B - the male fledged in 1982 and female fledged in 1983.

'Sometimes the fly-off parent soars quickly up to 1,000 feet and does an aerial recce of where to feed that's suitable,' says a note I wrote that day. The chick would come to greet the incoming parent, on one occasion going under a single-stranded wire fence to do so – despite the parents being wary of the fence.

On 11th July, John Hampshire left a note saying 'We have lift-off. JH.' The young crane had fledged at exactly ten weeks old. This first successful breeding for this pair of cranes was when the female was five years old and the male six. This pairing also shows that siblings can be fertile and successfully produce young.

So at the end of summer 1988, there were seven cranes at Horsey:

1 and 2: Pair A, consisting of the original male and female that arrived in September 1979.
3 and 4: this year's successful Pair B, both offspring of Pair A, the male youngster raised in 1982 and the female that fledged in 1983.
5: a migrant that arrived, firstly at Hickling, in November 1985 as a bird of that year but not, apparently, bred locally.
6: a bird reared by Pair A (1 & 2 above) in the summer of 1986, with the fifth bird becoming pair C.
7: the young bird fledged this year, 1988, by Pair B (3 and 4 above). It was probably a female, but this was not deduced until later when it was seen to be smaller than the migrant that arrived in 1991, eventually to be part of pair D.

Cranes? No, none here.

An additional story from the mid-1980s, told by Richard Hobbs to Chris Durdin in 2013.

Secrecy may have been the best way to safeguard the cranes in the early years, but they could be tricky birds to hide. This dilemma was illustrated by the visit of a group of conservation students to Norfolk Wildlife Trust's Hickling nature reserve in about 1985. Richard Hobbs, then the Trust's Conservation Officer, was with them. John Buxton from Horsey was also there, with Christopher Cadbury from Hickling who was a generous benefactor of Hickling reserve and Horsey Estate's crane protection.

One of the students was alert to the sound of calling cranes coming from nearby Horsey. He pointed them out with some confidence as he came from Sweden and heard cranes there regularly. John and Christopher simply denied it, and the student looked perplexed. Richard, a leading figure in the local conservation scene, knew about the cranes' return to Horsey, and after John and Christopher departed confirmed to the student that he was right.

This recalls an account of John's where he was quizzed about cranes by a birdwatcher and he batted that away by talking about the mechanical cranes on the shoreline doing sea defence work. We don't know if that birdwatcher knew John was spinning a line or thought he was potty!

Chapter 4
The lean years – and a failed experiment at captive-rearing 1989 – 1996

1989

Two pairs nested this year, as in 1988. Pair A failed, Pair B probably hatched a chick, but failed by late June.

Two more birds were also present this spring and summer, roosting at night at Chapman's Marsh at Hickling. In July, an additional crane joined the group. It appeared to be an adult or near-adult bird from the well-marked pattern of white on the head and neck. This bird reappeared in August and tried to join the main group and was often chased away. It persisted, and became part of the group in autumn and winter. A crane fitting the description of this one was seen at Cley in north Norfolk on 15th November, so its disappearance and reappearance may be real, due to it wandering, rather than simply slipping from view in the Horsey area. The winter group numbered nine, which in hindsight is puzzling as by calculation there were only eight we could account for, suggesting another migrant had joined them.

The highlight of this year was to watch an egg being laid by the female of Pair A, at their second or third attempt. The action took place on the nest that I had re-built in 1987. Incidentally, greylag geese nested on it and reared young in 1988.

This is how it was recorded in the Estate's notebooks, dated 10th May 1989. At the top of the page, written later, it says, 'Very special event – old crane lays first egg.' The account then says:

> 'Young crane of 1988 was in the area and the old pair came on later to a reed pond. They went there from feeding on spuds nearby. 8 pm I saw the old pair fly to the reed pond from another hide so went carefully to the hide, which viewed onto this pond. There they were, the female on my nest, which I had re-upholstered three days before with a fresh supply of dead reeds.'
>
> 'She was on the nest and he was a few yards to the right on the edge of the island. He was growling most of the time, a very low noise that I have only heard when they are near the nest. She answered him with low croaks, a quiet noise, not audible at any distance, I think. Very quiet conditions, no wind, so ideal for sound effects, which I hope I got on ¼ inch tape. She was standing on the nest as the light went at 8:15; too dark to photograph now anyway. She kept looking down and very particularly pecking and poking at the material and fussily putting little bits of reed back and forth near her feet.'

'Then she began to stoop down on her 'hocks', and up again. Then, after more poking and pecking again, from a semi-sitting position was turning round slowly as if to even out the centre of the nest, with her weight evenly on the whole length of her feet plus lower leg to the joint.'

'8:30. I noticed with a telescope (24 magnification) that when her tail end was towards my view that the short feathers by her cloaca were fluttering. Then once more up again she stood, full height, and looked about while he went on growling from his position about ten yards away.'

'Then she slowly lowered herself again and stayed down on her hocks for about two minutes. Then up quickly and immediately reached down from the fully standing position with her beak straight down and there was an egg which she gently prodded and rolled between her feet! She looked at it hard as if to say "Goodness, did I really produce that?"

'She then slowly stood up again and even more delicately stepped round with the egg between her feet and, looking down from on high with her beak close to the egg, moving her head round half a circle then the other way. After about five minutes of this she very slowly sank down on the egg, fluffed up her feathers as she sat firmly onto it and incubation began.'

'A really incredible sight to have witnessed and made me feel really pleased that I had helped in setting up this unique situation. The light was now too low to really see well so I left them at it after a further quarter of an hour. And she had got up once or twice and adjusted the egg again. The male had remained about the same place all the time, just apparently giving encouraging growls.'

It seemed as if she was as surprised as I was that she had produced the egg. Three days later, when the male was incubating:

'13th May. Terrific thunderstorm in the afternoon. I was in the hide and witnessed the male, the old crane, incubating while the rain poured off his beak end. He did well and sat it out.'

On 14th May, Pair A was doing fine and two eggs were seen on the early morning watch. On the morning of 15th May, I overslept and missed the morning watch. The account says:

'Horrors: the old pair was on the flood marsh, seen from the main hide, and there was obviously something wrong. I went to the pond hide. EMPTY NEST. I checked the nest by wading out there and found no sign of human intrusion; I'm certain it would have shown. Late evening: no clues and a real mystery, no sign of the eggs at all or shells, they had been physically removed by something.'

On the following day, 16th May:

'I went early morning. There was no sign of any cranes. I walked towards Horsey Mere and heard a rustle in the wet reed marsh [about 100 yards from where the nest had been], and saw a fox galloping out of the growing reed, which was about a foot deep in water. The fox looked back at 150 yards but all I had was a .22 with a silencer, useless at that range. How infuriating and so very disappointing after such a tremendous coup to have the old pair nesting there at last. I am sure that the partly amphibious fox took the eggs.'

Following the loss of the cranes' eggs at the reed pond nest, on two occasions I placed a goose egg in a specially created 'nest' near the reed pond hide. The purpose of this was to see if I could observe the culprit, which I presumed to be the fox, in the act of taking an egg. Both goose eggs disappeared overnight, which meant any chance of shooting the fox was lost, and more or less ruled out human intervention as the cause of the cranes' failure.

Having failed, Pair A nested again, to my surprise east of the main road between Somerton and Horsey Mill. The nest was in a narrow strip of reed, about 12 feet wide, between two ditches with open cattle-grazed marshes either side. Though the nest was not visible from the road, it would have been possible to watch the birds come and go. This was the only occasion that cranes nested east of the road. By 26th June, the pair was roosting together at Mere Farm, suggesting this attempt had petered out. I visited the nest in early July, finding two halves of an eggshell, suggesting it had hatched but the chick had been lost to a predator.

1990

Pair A disappeared during snow and did not return. Pair B failed, losing a chick once in June and possibly again in July.

Cranes moving away from Horsey in bad weather is typical behaviour. It was, at first, intriguing that the failure of the original pair to return this year coincided with a pair of cranes nesting in Normandy, France. We learnt about this in a letter from Michel Métais of La Ligue pour la Protection des Oiseaux (LPO) to Chris Durdin, and we then understood that this was their first nest in France since the 19th century, prompting the thought that these birds could be our Pair A. It later came to light that a pair of cranes had been breeding successfully in that area since 1985, just three years after the first young fledged at Horsey. Though this meant we didn't find out what happened to our original pair, knocking on the head the neat and tidy notion that they had simply moved to France, it was further evidence of cranes' westward spread.

Spoonbill at Horsey, spring 1989.

Events this year highlighted the debate on how secret or otherwise our cranes really were, as they attempted to nest for the tenth successive year.

The report, in The Times of 24th April 1990, that cranes were nesting in the UK provoked a minor storm. The Times journalist thought breeding cranes was a good story, saying that their presence "… was the most closely guarded secret of the decade".

This followed the period, during 1988 and 1989, when the book *Red Data Birds in Britain* was in preparation. Written by a team from the then Nature Conservancy Council (NCC) and the RSPB, this new book was the British version of international Red Data Books about endangered, vulnerable or rare species. Naturally the authors, Leo Batten and Peter Clement of the NCC and Colin Bibby, Graham Elliott and Richard Porter of the RSPB, wished to include crane in the book. Draft texts were prepared; I was consulted and was happy with the content, which carefully avoided saying where the cranes were nesting. The book was published by T & A D Poyser in autumn 1990.

The Horsey Estate and the RSPB had successfully suppressed publicity about cranes over the previous 10 years. Suppressed is a strong word, but fair in this context. Nonetheless, the regular wintering flock of cranes in the Horsey area was well known in the birdwatching community, and indeed noted in annual Norfolk Bird Reports. The appearance of obviously juvenile cranes in this group meant that it was steadily becoming better known that they were breeding at Horsey, so to include cranes in *Red Data Birds in Britain* was a natural step. Wider publicity was another matter.

I was furious as I was under the impression that there was a meeting between The Times and RSPB staff about the book. Recalling this period, Richard Porter, then Head of Species Protection at the RSPB, is clear that there was no such meeting. He was well aware of how this would have upset me, knew that the cranes were being well protected by the Estate and that it remained common sense that the RSPB's involvement should stay at arms' length. My reaction illustrates how protective I felt towards the cranes, which overall served them well.

I blamed the RSPB for releasing the information with poor timing during the nesting season, and my wife Bridget fired off an angry letter to RSPB Director Ian Prestt. Ian visited Horsey, with his brother and sister-in-law, and with characteristic skill poured oil on troubled waters and good relations were restored.

By contrast, the RSPB warden at Horsey in 1990, Jerry Tanguay, wrote in his end of season report that the Times was wrong in its description of a "closely guarded secret". He offered the view that the visitor was "… right who said on June 3rd that people knew the cranes had been there for ten years and are likely to be for some time and that therefore they were in no hurry to see them".

On the ground, there was no impact from the mention in The Times. It appeared that Pair B's chick hatched on around 16th June, and the parents were observed being attentive on 20th June. But two days later they were free of parental duties, the youngster presumably having been lost to a predator, and they were clearly seen without a chick on 25th June.

John Hampshire was doing the night shift, often watching from Stubb Mill. On 19th July he suspected another chick was there, and on 20th July the cranes' behaviour again suggested there might be a chick, but this came to nothing. In hindsight, hatching a second chick so quickly is highly unlikely, taking into account the typical 30-day incubation period. If a chick was lost later on 20th June, then even allowing for a short incubation of just 28 days, for a chick to be hatched by 19th July means the egg would have been laid on 21st June, the day after the previous chick was lost. The cranes were seen on and off to the year-end.

1991

The first year with three pairs, two of which nested. Pair B pair hatched one young, at least, but it was thought to have been lost to a fox. Pair C also nested in the remote marsh area. Pair D did not attempt to nest and a seventh bird, an immature, arrived in March 1991.

The cranes left Horsey on 7th February in hard weather, one returning on 23rd February then four on 25th February. On 23rd March, a new young crane was seen at Mere Farm, Horsey, where it fed with another immature bird, the latter almost certainly the 1988 youngster. The new crane had a completely brown head and neck, so was certainly a young bird from last year, 1990. We know none was produced locally, so presumably it had been seen off by its parents somewhere else. At the time, the thought came to mind that it could be a young bird from what we thought could be our Pair A in Normandy. We learnt later that this idea was wrong: a Scandinavian migrant slightly off-course is most likely. It was taller than the 1988 youngster, so was probably a male.

On 25th March, all seven cranes were together. Notes made at the time show it was getting increasingly difficult to recognise them as individuals.

This was the first year that Pair C nested, this pair consisting of a young bird raised locally in 1986 by Pair A and a migrant that arrived in 1985. It was first of this pair's 11 years of failure even to hatch an egg.

The nests of the two active pairs were not more than 300 yards apart, but both petered out just after the due hatching date. There were four nests of marsh harriers and two of bitterns in the marsh where the cranes were nesting; perhaps harriers accounted for the failure of the fertile pair.

Visitors to Horsey in 1991 included the Earl of Cranbrook, Chairman of English Nature, Lady Caroline Cranbrook and Bill Makins of Pensthorpe Waterfowl Park in April, and English Nature's Dr Leo Batten and Bill Makins again in September. Discussions were underway about actively intervening to help the cranes.

1992 – The Pensthorpe experiment
Three pairs of cranes nested at Horsey for the first time.
Four eggs (two clutches) were taken from Pair B, which then did not re-lay again.
Two eggs taken from Pair C went to Pensthorpe and were proved to be infertile.
A third pair, Pair D, attempted to nest, the fourth pair of cranes to have nested at Horsey.
No eggs were taken from these, but they lost their single chick, probably to a fox, when it was about three weeks old.

By the end of 1990, I was worried about the cranes' failure to produce many young. By careful observation and noting their behaviour I calculated, in January 1991, that cranes had laid a total of 30 eggs at Horsey over a period of ten years. From these, just four young had fledged. This struck me as an unnecessary waste, and that it was time for some human assistance for these very special birds, taking steps beyond predator control and many hours of observation.

The idea came to mind of trying to bypass the stages of eggs and small young, which were so vulnerable to predators. At this time, it felt like the whole re-colonisation process might falter. Some help for the cranes would, at least, speed the process of expansion.

Incubating and rearing young birds came to mind and it was suggested that we could use the facilities and expertise at Pensthorpe Waterfowl Park near Fakenham in Norfolk. We made contact with Bill Makins, the then owner and driving force behind Pensthorpe, who was immediately enthusiastic about the idea and agreed to help.

Taking eggs from wild birds can only be done under licence so the approval of English Nature was needed. My cousin Aubrey Buxton, who had served on English Nature's Council, kindly raised this idea with English Nature chairman the Earl of Cranbrook, leading to Dr Leo Batten overseeing the project. The outcome was that a licence was applied for in March 1992 to take up to six eggs 'to enhance breeding success of [a] tiny population of cranes, which is heavily predated in the egg and nestling stages'. The application set out that incubation would be in a rearing pen at Pensthorpe, followed by a release pen at Horsey over a period of approximately three months to acclimatise the birds in the release area.

The RSPB was consulted about the proposal and was less than enthusiastic, but accepted that it should be feasible and went along with the experiment on the understanding that it was to be supervised by the statutory conservation bodies. English Nature duly granted the licence.

'Up to six eggs' was proposed, so potentially up to two eggs from each pair could be taken for captive rearing, knowing that cranes quickly re-lay following the loss of eggs. We took the first clutch of two eggs from Pair B on 2nd May. Though they hatched, the tiny chicks did not survive. We then took a clutch of two eggs from Pair C on 9th May, which proved to be infertile. This alerted us to a problem with this pair; subsequently they proved to be permanently infertile and failed to hatch any young despite nesting every year for 11 years (1991-2001 inclusive). In 2002, we found the male of this pair dead and a post-mortem showed lead pellets that may have caused this infertility.

The third pair (Pair D) at Horsey this year was a new nesting pair, consisting of one bird that had arrived on migration pairing with, we believe, the young bird fledged at Horsey in 1986. I concluded it was unwise to disturb their first nesting attempt in case this should put them off for the future. They produced a chick that reached three weeks old. I regularly saw a fox in the area of the nest but failed to shoot it, so this was the likeliest culprit for the loss of the chick.

So the decision was taken to take a second clutch of two eggs from the sibling Pair B, which had re-laid within ten days at a new nest. This we did on 22nd May. The pair stayed at Horsey, but did not re-lay for a third time. These two eggs were taken to Pensthorpe and, using artificial incubation, one failed and one hatched. The crane chick was raised successfully, but it became imprinted on the people feeding it – that is to say recognising people as its parents rather than cranes.

That crane chick came to Horsey on 21st August where it was kept in a roofed release pen, about 20 yards square. This had been built on the marsh adjacent to regular crane feeding areas, close to where Pair D had nested and lost their single chick that spring. Within a day of that loss, I had seen them crossing a dyke to have a better look at a pair of greylag geese, as if they mistook them for their lost youngster. I also recall the crane pair calling mournfully, as if they were grieving their loss some ten days before.

From a hide, I saw this adult pair come up to the release pen and attempt to make contact with the one-month-old Pensthorpe-reared chick. This was the first time it had seen adult cranes and on seeing them the chick looked alarmed and fled to the opposite side of the pen.

It was tempting to go to the pen and open the door to release the chick but I resisted due to the reaction of the young crane to the adults. After the adults had left the area, I went over to feed the chick. It was delighted to see me as usual and fed happily at my feet on the pellets I provided.

The young crane, a female, was returned to Pensthorpe in November 1992, where she remains to this day. I was delighted to meet her again in 2008 when Bill and Deb Jordan, by now the owners of Pensthorpe Nature Reserve, kindly invited my wife Bridget and me to a small gathering with George Archibald, who was visiting Pensthorpe. It was a happy reunion. In front of their lovely house was a pair of common cranes strutting up and down on the lawn, only 30 yards from us. The female was this hand-reared chick from the egg taken from Horsey. It was a most moving moment for me to recall the story of this female crane, now 16 years old.

The experiment had failed and was not repeated. There was some correspondence in 1995 about trying captive breeding again with the help of the Wildfowl & Wetlands Trust, but this did not attract support and came to nothing.

Eventually, wild cranes bred successfully again at Horsey in 1997, five years after the Pensthorpe experiment, and in subsequent years, so captive breeding, always controversial, became unneces-sary as numbers in east Norfolk began to grow steadily. By contrast, the idea of captive breeding has recently gained support in nature conservation circles, notably with the return of red kites to several parts of Britain and white-tailed eagles in Scotland, and now the reintroduction of cranes to the Somerset Levels and Moors through The Great Crane Project.

I admit to mixed feelings about The Great Crane Project. It's partly the name. There was a press report with a picture labelled a 'Great Crane': I fear the project's name may confuse some people and a new species name will come into use. It also takes away from the fact that we have had a great crane project underway in the Broads for several decades. I am relieved that The Great Crane Project is well away from the cranes' slow but successful and natural re-colonisation of eastern England. Yet when Sir Peter Scott came to witness the cranes at Horsey in 1985 he mentioned to me at the time that it would be wonderful if they could be introduced to Slimbridge and the West Country one day. I understand that emotion, which must motivate Peter's Wildfowl & Wetlands Trust in particular.

1993
All three pairs nested, and all failed.

Pair B hatched a chick 20th May, as deduced from their change of activity. They could be heard while walking in an area of saw-sedge cut short the previous autumn: a low croak from the adult and a high 'peeping' from a single chick. These are both quiet, subtle sounds, only heard from within 50 yards. The chick had been lost by 2nd June.

Pair C we now knew to be infertile, so again failed.

Pair D produced an egg that did not hatch, discovered on checking the nest on 28th June with Robin Lang, the National Trust warden. English Nature granted a licence on 29th June: "To take by hand for scientific purposes the addled or deserted eggs of crane (*Grus grus*) as found in the county of Norfolk." On 2nd July, the addled egg was taken by the RSPB's Peter Newbery and passed for analysis to Monks Wood, the research station in Cambridgeshire run by the Institute of Terrestrial Ecology (ITE). No abnormally high levels of toxic residues were found (ITE *pers comm* to Peter Newbery).

This year, there were seven nests of marsh harriers on the Horsey Estate. In November nine cranes were reported together, including two additional migrants that stayed through the winter.

1994

Three pairs nested, but all were believed to have failed.

Lord Cranbrook, still chairman of English Nature, visited with Lady Caroline Cranbrook on 5th March, when all nine birds were seen together. He was 'duly impressed', as the notebook of the time says. Two of the nests were estimated to be just 150 yards apart, the closest nests recorded at Horsey. Other human 'visitors' this spring led to the only prosecution linked to cranes, described in Chapter 10.

It is worth noting estimated laying dates, in view of the dates the following year. Pair B, from their behaviour, laid on 25th April. Pair C laid on about 28th April, close to a harriers' nest. No laying dates were noted for Pair D, nesting just off the Horsey Estate this year, but they reached the chick stage for the first time before being predated. The fourth pair and the remaining single bird appeared to have left the area by late April.

On 30th April, something was clearly wrong with Pair C. They twice flew back to the nest site, giving alarm calls most of the time, then eventually they flew off westwards. The nest had plainly been disturbed. On checking it, there were broken eggshells, from a single egg, but certainly no signs of human interference.

On 8th May, both birds from Pair B flew away from the nest to feed on arable fields, suggesting they too had failed. They started nesting again and were noted to have laid an egg by 20th May, a maximum of just 12 days after the first egg or clutch had been lost. This nesting attempt petered out but pair D, well to the south, probably hatched their first chick on 5th May and was seen feeding it on 12th June. This chick had gone when I returned from filming in Northumberland on 17th June. There were no foxes or fox droppings in that area, pointing to marsh harriers as possible predators.

Chasing off greylag geese.

An interesting observation on 16th May involved an aerial chase by a crane of a pair of greylag geese. The likeliest reason for the chase is to move geese away from the nest. Greylag geese nests are very similar to those of cranes – indeed eggs of greylags and cranes are the same size – so there must be a risk that geese could take over a crane's nest if not discouraged.

The cranes may have been unsuccessful, but it was the first successful year for avocets at Horsey; four pairs fledged a total of 15 chicks. It was a good year too for ruffs: reeves – female ruffs – peaked at 210 on 2nd May with two definite male ruffs present as well, though there is there no suggestion that they bred, and a spoonbill was also present in late May.

1995
For the fourth successive year, three pairs failed to fledge any chicks.

Just the three pairs over-wintered. Though three pairs failed to fledge any chicks, Pair D, nesting just south of the Horsey Estate, again reached the chick stage. Until this year, the usual egg-laying date was during the third week of April, but all three pairs laid much earlier, on 1st, 3rd and 5th April. This contrasts with the first full boom of a bittern on the typical date of 2nd April.

The obvious conclusion is that this must have been a warm spring, but that's far from clear from the nearest Met Office data set, for Lowestoft. April 1995 was the warmest April of the 1990s, but with average temperatures (the 6th of the 11 years 1990-2000). The weather in March is more likely to be an influence. It was the sunniest March of the decade, though temperatures were average, and it was the second wettest March of the decade. Perhaps the combination of sunshine and high water levels after rain prompted early egg-laying.

A new immature bird was seen in two places on 13th April. Notes at the time recorded it as a first-summer bird with very little black and white apparent on the head and neck. This bird had not been seen the previous winter, so presumably was a migrant. It was not seen again at Horsey.

1996
Two pairs – Pairs B and C – failed, with Pair B trying twice. But where was Pair D?

Curiously, there is no record of Pair D this year – the pair that moved away from Horsey in 2001. It is possible that they nested and details are in a missing notebook. However, a landowner in another Broadland river valley recalls a pair of cranes being present around this time.

Sheep fencing was put up alongside much of the fen, through which cranes are unable to walk onto the grazing marsh, and the owners of this could not be persuaded to move it, having made their investment. The cranes shifted their nesting sites in the fen the following year, suggesting that they were well aware of the fence as a barrier.

This was the final year of a run of eight years, 1989 to 1996, with a consistent population of two or three pairs, but not a single young crane fledged. The growth of the population was not to start until 1997 – as described in the next chapter.

Forty avocets arrived onto the 'scrape' at Horsey, March 1996 (here with black-tailed godwits).

Chapter 5
Cranes on the up
1997 – 2006

1997
Three pairs produced two – or maybe four – young.

This year was quite a turning point as, after eight years of failure, there was a huge step forward with four pairs. These certainly fledged two young, but there is a strong possibility that in fact four young were locally produced. One or possibly two additional birds also over-summered.

Pair D was successful at their first attempt: two tiny chicks were videoed on 9th May, suggesting eggs were laid in early April. Pair C failed, infertile, as in every year since 1991. A fourth pair – Pair E – were hanging around close to Pair D, but so far as we know did not nest this year.

The outcome from Pair B is uncertain. We assumed they had failed, and two juvenile cranes seen on 6th December were at the time thought to be migrants, which is how they are recorded in *The Birds of Norfolk* and in the Norfolk Bird Report of that year. However, two years later, in 1999, two young cranes were fledged by Pair B, which then as in 1997 nested in the saw-sedge fen in part of the estate that can only be reached by boat. In 1997, they were watched infrequently after June. We will probably never know for sure, but this raises the intriguing possibility that the additional juvenile birds seen in December 1997 were also raised at Horsey, but overlooked. Another possibility is that cranes nested successfully in the other Broadland river valley and the family party joined the main group for the winter, but this seems less likely as it was Pair D that moved away from Horsey to breed in 2001, and they certainly nested at Horsey in 1997.

So, if four chicks fledged successfully this year, the most since cranes first nested in 1981, why did previously unsuccessful pairs succeed this year?

Four factors could affect the ability of cranes to fledge young successfully. The condition of the adult birds, related to winter food supply, food supply in spring /summer for chicks and adults, timing of nesting and predation. Food supply in winter is unlikely to be a factor, as the supply of potatoes provided for the cranes is consistent year to year. Food supply in spring/summer is more difficult to measure. It appears that chicks have been produced on numerous occasions, but they often die at around three weeks old, at a stage when their food demands are increasing rapidly. However, there was nothing notable about 1997 that suggests this was a factor, or indeed is ever a constraint. Cranes at Horsey have had many failures and successes both from broods laid early or from later re-lays. Lack of predation is probably the key factor, perhaps aided by a little luck.

Pair B moved its nest site this year. As noted earlier, sheep fencing was put up in 1996 alongside much of the fen where this pair always nested, making it impossible for any chick to walk onto the grazing marshes to feed in that area. Presumably as a consequence of that, they moved their nesting site to a new location within easy walking distance of grazing marshes to the north. The new nest was not itself more secure, but just by being in a different place it is likely to have made it more difficult for the canny local foxes to find them.

This year's success was a turning point for cranes in the Broads. It also meant that captive breeding ideas for cranes at Horsey, at least, were shelved permanently.

Remarkably, there was also a probable breeding attempt in Scotland this year. As at Horsey, those in the know kept it quiet, and it wasn't until 2007 that this pair, in Caithness, became public. It seems likely that there may be, or have been, other pairs of cranes elsewhere in the UK, in the first decade of the 21st century especially, and that information about these will, over time, come to light.

1998
Four pairs produced one young.

Pair D hatched twins. A fox was seen near them on 20th June; all four birds were seen several times on 23rd June. One chick had gone by 26th June, so the fox is the likeliest predator. But this pair did successfully fledge one young, unlike the other three pairs, which all failed. Pair D had black bustles so were easy to distinguish from Pair E, both of which had grey bustles. Pair E was probably a male that was Pair B's first offspring in 1998 with a female that arrived as a young bird in 1991. They nested for the first time, just off the Horsey Estate to the south, which became their normal pattern.

1999
Four pairs at or adjacent to Horsey for a third year, producing two young. Pair B raised two chicks, and the other three pairs failed.

It wasn't until mid-December that two young from Pair B were seen on West Craft marshes. The Estate notebook records that I had been so busy watching Pair D that I never seriously watched the fen after June though I had heard unison calls throughout summer. Pair E again nested just outside the Horsey Estate and probably laid eggs on around 26th April, but they gave up and moved off, including feeding at Heigham Holmes, from around 12th May.

2000
Four pairs, all failed to raise any young.

Eleven birds were present all year, made up of the four pairs, two chicks raised in 1999 and a single bird, perhaps the bird raised in 1998. Pair B was seen chaperoning a chick or chicks until 6th July, but not subsequently. Pair E was again just outside the Horsey boundary but my diary records that they "never really got going". We assume they attempted to nest but this was not confirmed.

Over the course of the winter there was a programme of conservation work on the southern part of the estate, grant-aided by English Nature, which included digging out dykes and the removal of trees and bushes in the marsh.

Black bustles on this pair.

2001

Four pairs of cranes, one of which moved away from Horsey where they fledged two young. Three pairs remaining at Horsey failed.

This year saw a major step in the crane story with successful breeding in another river valley in the Broads, which has had at least one pair of cranes every year since then. Pair D first failed at Horsey, before moving to the new area, where they fledged two young. The family of four returned to the Horsey area to join the winter flock. This was the first time breeding was confirmed away from Horsey since historical times, starting with a major success. It's perhaps surprising that this occurred two years before cranes took the shorter journey to nest at Hickling within the Thurne broads and marshes area.

At Horsey, Pair B failed and Pair C also failed, as usual. Pair E nested just outside the Horsey boundary and produced two chicks, which they brought onto Horsey, but one was lost in late July aged about eight weeks. A dropping from a Chinese water deer was found very near a failed nest this year; something similar was seen in a previous year. Could they be taking eggs?

Chinese water deer.

2002
Three pairs nested at Horsey, without success, and two dead cranes.

It was a year with two crane corpses that prompted post mortems. At Horsey, Pair B failed. Pair C, having nested unsuccessfully since 1986, finally split up and the male was found dead. Pair E apparently tried to nest within the Horsey Estate but finally chose to nest outside our boundary. Pair D nested again in another river valley, and again raised two chicks.

The first of the two dead cranes that went for post mortem was a migrant, rather than one of the Horsey birds. In about March 2002, the RSPCA hospital at East Winch telephoned to ask if any cranes had been lost from Horsey. A crane at Orfordness in Suffolk had been caught in a ditch with a landing net. The bird was weak, unable to fly and was lame with a displaced hip. At this stage, the male from Pair B at Horsey was lame and had gone missing so it seemed possible this was a Horsey bird, though not likely that it should have gone so far in poor health. The RSPCA asked for help in finding accommodation for the crane. Joe Blossom, former treasurer of the Wildfowl & Wetlands Trust, had tame cranes at his house at Calthorpe near Hickling, and he agreed to take in the bird, which sadly died after two days. The next day, out at Horsey with Joe, there was the missing Horsey crane, looking less lame!

The dead crane, presumably a migrant, was taken to the Westover Veterinary Centre in North Walsham, where vet Louise Rayment kindly did a post mortem free of charge, described as 'cosmetic' so that the skin could be kept for taxidermy. Her report, dated 25th April 2002, says that the post mortem 'revealed extensive fungal plaques believed to be caused by *Aspergillus* spp. It is definitely the cause of death in this bird and due to being so extensive, no further investigations were undertaken.' The mounted bird is at Horsey Hall.

A second dead crane was found in September 2002, thought to be one of the infertile Pair C. Vet Louise Rayment again performed a post mortem examination, on 20th January 2003. Her report, dated 11th February 2003, notes correctly that the carcass had been frozen and that lesions to the neck area were believed to be due to predation after death.

> 'The bird was in less than perfect condition and the breast bone was quite prominent indicating that it had been ill for some time. There was a history of the bird showing a lameness affecting the left leg ... there was a mass attached to the left leg and evidence of shotgun pellets affecting other areas of the carcass. The shotgun pellets were few in number and would not have been the direct cause of death.'

The post mortem, which established that the bird was a male, went on to say that the liver, spleen and kidneys were affected with multiple abscesses caused by avian tuberculosis. The lead shot may well have explained the permanent infertility of this pair.

Now mounted and at Horsey Hall, this migrant was found dead in March 2002.

2003
Two pairs nested at Horsey, and a nest at Hickling for the first time.

A successful year with the first breeding at Hickling, two young produced at Horsey and two more young cranes joining the group. A pair at Hickling successfully raised one young within an open block of reed, cut annually. Not surprisingly, the Norfolk Wildlife Trust chose to keep their presence quiet. Looking at them at Horsey in September, they appeared to be a new breeding pair.

At Horsey, Pair B nested in the fen and produced one young that was seen aged one month old. These birds were difficult to follow and we were uncertain about the final outcome until this pair and a chick were seen on the main flood on 3rd September. Pair E courted at Horsey then disappeared in early April. They reappeared as a pair on 20th May, then just a single bird from about 3rd June suggesting the other was sitting on a nest. A single chick from the nest just off the estate was brought back to Horsey and the family roosted on Robin's Flood. The chick successfully fledged on 10th September when the family flew a short distance together.

Pair D courted at Horsey but nested away. Two more young cranes that fledged in another Broadland river valley arrived to join the resident group after the breeding season.

2004
Two pairs nested at Horsey, neither fledged young.

Though Horsey was becoming less crucial for breeding cranes, observations this year showed it still has a central role out of the breeding season, in combination with other areas in the Upper Thurne. On 30th January, 27 cranes were on a farm at Hickling, then 21 cranes at Heigham Holmes on 3rd February. On the Horsey Estate, the potato pile maintained as a crane feeding site was attracting other wildlife: 16 red deer on 12th February, made up of 13 hinds and calves and three stags; on 15th February, 21 cranes; then on 18th February there were 12 cranes and a few greylag geese.

Red deer.

Pair D, recognisable by their black bustles and again nesting away from the Thurne Valley, was on the potatoes on 13th and 15th April. In the evening of 15th April, Pair E chased off the other five cranes at Horsey.

Both of the two pairs at Horsey showed signs of incubating, but we don't know if any young were hatched and certainly no young fledged. Pair E's nest was again adjacent to Horsey. Unusually, Pair B first tried in its usual saw-sedge marsh, then attempted in another site, but without success. By 15th June, there were already seven cranes roosting on the main flood and two others on Robin's Flood.

A pair nested at Hickling, for a second year, on a pile of reed litter left over from winter reed cutting in clear view of the Bittern Hide. This new hide was shut on the pretence of subsidence, which was ineffective in keeping their presence quiet, and nest watches were instigated, during which a fox was watched approaching the nest and seen off by the adults. One young fledged and returned to Horsey on 31st August to form a group, now numbering 16.

2005
Two pairs nested at Horsey, one pair fledging one young.

An observation in the Horsey Estate notebook from 28th April 2005 points to young cranes doing a 'migration spiral' but with nowhere to go.

> 'Warm and clear, SW slight breeze. I heard cranes calling with soaring migration flight croaks. There was a pair [on the marsh below] answering. High up in the sky circling east there were three lots of two cranes and a single bird close to them – seven in total. The two took off from the marsh and quickly climbed in circles to join them at approximately 1500 feet, all calling to each other and enjoying the sensation of the moment! What a view they must have up there. After minutes of flying, all nine descended slowly to the Heigham Holmes area and a pair peeled off to Robin's Flood and reed marsh and the calling ceased.'

The following day, 29th April, I watched Pair B doing an incubation handover, confirming they were nesting successfully. Elsewhere, eight birds were seen at roost on 2nd May, including Pair E, suggesting they had tried to nested and failed or not yet attempted to breed. But by 2nd June it was clear that Pair E had successfully settled adjacent to Horsey. On 19th June I saw them with a tiny chick, perhaps about one week old, and on 21st June, I could see they had twins. I made their roosting nest a bit higher on 25th June and they used it the following night. On 1st August, I received a message while I was away in Norway that "your two feathered grandchildren are fine" at age 8½ weeks, meaning those two chicks. But by 8th August, when I was back at Horsey, there was just one chick with the pair on grazing marshes opposite the fen, another reminder that they are vulnerable to predators until they can fly.

This year was the first and only occasion, so far, when there were two pairs at Hickling, from which four hatched and two fledged.

2006
Two pairs at Horsey, but no chicks fledged.

At Horsey, there were two nesting pairs of cranes, though often many more cranes present, including a group of 15 feeding on potatoes on 15th May. As numbers increased, we had largely given up on the increasingly difficult task of keeping track of which pair was which, though it is likely that Pair B continued to nest in the saw-sedge marsh until at least 2010, with Pair E nesting in the southern part of the estate or immediately adjacent to Horsey.

The second pair at Horsey nested within the now fenced area round the main flood, the scrape we formed by extending an old flight pond. They settled around 29th May, were off the nest on 2nd June and re-laid between 6th and 10th June. On 13th June, one of the fenced-in cranes was videoed swallowing a duckling six inches long. These cranes would not fly out, preferring to feed on what they could find on the flood – including being filmed taking a large avocet chick. Neither Horsey pair fledged chicks.

A juvenile present from 23rd September to 12th October was thought to be fledged from the pair now established in Yorkshire. It was last seen in Yorkshire on 20th September, which supports this idea. In other years when young were fledged in Yorkshire, the circumstantial evidence that they came to Horsey is poorer. DNA analysis will be needed to prove any link as migrant juveniles in east Norfolk are also possible.

Crane family on their night roost, 28th June 2005.

At Hickling, the Wildlife Trust gave up on trying to keep the cranes' presence a secret and erected an old hide on the edge of the block of cut reed on which the birds were nesting, allowing the public and volunteers to watch the nest. From here, one morning in May, a fox was seen at the nest; it appeared at first to have been seen off by the female crane but not for long as the birds did not return to the nest site. They hung around between five and ten yards from the nest, preening and calling loudly and then flew off to adjacent marshes. When the nest was visited later that day it was empty with no trace of eggs.

Chapter 6
Recent crane diaries 2007 – 2013

In recent years I have kept more detailed diaries again, partly with this book in mind. These have concentrated on the pair of cranes in the southern part of the Horsey Estate where access is easy and a homemade hide allows close observation of the nesting area. Pairs of cranes nesting in the sedge fen have been allowed to get on their business without being watched over, and to judge fledging success we have relied on observations of the birds, with or without chicks, as they emerged onto adjacent open grazing marsh.

2007

One young bird, from a nest immediately adjacent to Horsey, spent much of its time as a chick at Horsey and fledged successfully; two other nests failed.

This year provides an illustration of how cranes nesting late can be successful, following earlier failures, and how crane habitats at Horsey link closely with adjacent areas. The latter reminds us that although we draw lines on maps to show who manages or owns land, the birds use the area as a whole. The expanding UK population was now at least ten pairs, including cranes in two counties away from Norfolk, yet the chick of the only successful pair this year largely grew up at Horsey.

My first diary notes, in March, refer to a pair of cranes possibly interested in nesting, but no courting seen. They were showing interest in a place in which they had not previously nested, a pond area in a reedbed, 500 yards from previous nesting sites. In early April, one pair seemed to be established with a definite nest site, but the main winter group of 19 birds was still together and were observed on reed stubble where the reed had been cut a month before. On 7th April, these 19 cranes were still roosting on a flood.

To encourage them to nest here, I built two dummy nests on the edge of the flooded area, hoping this would tempt them to take up residence, having done this before with success (see 1981 and 1987 accounts). A roosting platform, we learnt then, may later be used as a nest. However, they chose to nest instead in the reed stubble, albeit rapidly growing now, and unusually some 50 yards from any open water. Perhaps they were tempted by the plentiful supply of cut reed as easily accessible material to build their nest. From a hide I saw one egg in this nest, but they abandoned it.

The second nest at Horsey, in the fen to the north of the estate, was also unsuccessful as the young bird was lost at about one month old, most likely taken by a fox. One pair at Hickling also failed.

Success came, at last, from a nest just off the Horsey Estate, towards Martham. Although the nesting conditions were good there, the grazing marshes and pools at Horsey gave more feeding opportunities so the chick spent much of its early days with us, as in several previous years. On 2nd June, a single adult crane was feeding on grazing marsh near its own nest. This was the first sign of a single bird; we hoped this meant that the other bird of the pair was sitting. Then on 19th June, a pair of cranes was close to the roosting area with my two constructed nests. The pair appeared to be behaving protectively as if there was something invisible to me in the longer grass, at 500 yards range. Could it be a chick?

> '20th June – at last! A little 'goldie' showed between the adults. I was sure that this is the pair which had nested south of the Horsey reserve and had relocated to be adjacent to their favourite feeding area on grazing marsh and, as had happened in the past, they had taken up a night roost on one of the nests I had built two months ago.'

Grey-bustled pair with chick on their night roost, July 2007.

So although my artificial platforms weren't used to nest, they or the pool did draw in this pair and chick, and progress then was steady. On 21st June, at 7 pm, I saw the crane family disappear towards their night roost. On 3rd July, the young bird now had a greyer head and body, so the goldie nickname for golden-coloured chicks was no longer suitable. The crane family was there again on the roost on 11th July and 15th August but by the later date had started to feed some of the time beyond our grazing marshes, adjacent to the roost, moving farther west to Heigham Holmes.

> '25th August – 7.00pm Three cranes flying together westward from towards night roost site in daytime. Using binoulars at half-mile distance the middle

of the three is definitely brown-headed. We have LIFT OFF for sure. I went to the hide and observed the family on the flood. The young bird with brown head was final proof of success.'

This was a late fledging date, possibly resulting from disturbed first and even second attempts to nest in early summer, though the following year they would be later still. The family of three, including one now flying young bird, was part of a flock of 20 cranes on Robin's flood on 3rd September.

The surprise of 2007 was well away from Horsey, with cranes nesting at the RSPB's new Lakenheath Fen nature reserve in Suffolk for the first time. The process to change carrot fields into fens had started just 11 years before. There were two pairs of cranes and up to three additional cranes around the reserve at various dates during the spring and summer. One of these pairs laid two eggs and the other pair made a nest but probably did not lay eggs. The first pair was seen on 21st March and, during April, Site Manager Norman Sills stumbled across a nest, to his astonishment, during routine surveys.

Coming just before the opening of the reserve's new visitor centre, it led to a debate about whether their presence should be announced. As a good news story to celebrate the transformation of this part of the Fens, the opportunity to celebrate was too difficult to resist. One pair was in a remote part of the reserve and away from disturbance, but still was unsuccessful. The other pair was closer to paths, though part of the network of trails was closed while they were nesting. While it may be that an increase in visitor numbers following the opening of the new visitor centre and associated publicity was a factor in this pair's failure, the experience at Horsey suggests it would have been surprising for them to raise young successfully at their first attempt at Lakenheath Fen.

Did the cranes at Lakenheath Fen come from Horsey? The birds in the expanding group in east Norfolk were not all accounted for in 2007, so it would be natural to assume so. A report of a group of cranes seen south of Norwich encouraged that idea, but that group of nine, at Wood-ton, south Norfolk, was on 20th May, long after the Lakenheath Fen birds had arrived. The Broadland cranes had gone beyond the small numbers from which individual birds can all be recognised. True migrants in the Fens are probably more likely. The crane population in eastern Europe is increasing and their range is moving steadily westwards. An upsurge in Denmark is particularly striking, where they were absent as a breeding bird for 100 years until 1952. From three or four pairs confined to northern Jutland since the 1950s, a remarkable increase kicked off in the 1990s and by 2010 about 120 pairs were spread across the whole country.

The presence of cranes at Lakenheath Fen coincided with an influx of migrant cranes into the UK. In spring and summer 2007, following persistent easterlies and anti-cyclonic weather from late March to early May, cranes were seen in at least 60 locations – excluding the Norfolk Broads – throughout the UK. As well as a likely source for birds nesting in the Fens, this brings hope that the UK's crane population will slowly grow over the coming years, from a combination of locally fledged birds and migrants. In future years, DNA analysis may shed further light on the origins of British breeding cranes and movement between the Broads and other areas.

2008

Three pairs at Horsey, two of which nested, raising three chicks.

Our winter diary for 2007/08 refers to observing the family from last year roosting on the main flood from mid-February 2008, sometimes accompanied by a total of 28 other cranes. I was able to follow closely the progress of this family – later a pair of cranes – as they could be seen from our main hide, and my diary entries below trace their story.

> '25th March 08 – A pair of cranes is now regularly feeding on the grazing marsh near the main hide. Their bustles were held high and occasionally they danced and flapped into the air a few times. In the evening they normally stop feeding and prepare to fly off together to the night roost. On this occasion the female stuck her neck out and typically after a pause in this position she took off and flew towards the roost on her own. The male watched her go but did not follow her for at least three minutes, he then flew with a distinctive courting flight; a downward wing beat in slow motion, typically performed when he is flying near the nest site.'

Black-bustled pair, March 2008.

I had seen them mating on the grazing marsh a few days before. Since then the weather had been very cold with a short spell of snow a few inches deep, and frost at night.

> '11th April – The pair of cranes was heard unison-calling from the potential nest site, a small pond approximately 100 yards square in a reedbed where cranes had nested infrequently before.'

> '14th April – This pair was feeding on the marsh in daytime when they were heard making single calls of alarm, interspersed with unison calls, because five adult cranes flew low over them northward, followed five minutes later by another four that did the same. I presume these were a group of immature birds from the last few years back.'

> '20th April – This pair had chased off their young of 2007 and though it tried to come back to join them over a few weeks it had now become independent.'

> '1st May – The nest site was definite and in heavy rain showers I watched drips coming off the female's beak as she sat huddled on the rather scanty nest, while he stood nearby facing the weather and looking miserable.'

> '12th May – The male crane was in a different area, walking about with its bustles held high as if in distress mode. I went to the observation hide nearer their nest site and the female bird was making a plaintive "Where are you?" call and obviously upset. She was standing some yards from the actual nest.

> '15th May – The cranes have definitely left their nest and are feeding again together on the grazing marshes. Realising something had happened I visited the nest site in the reed stubble and found no sign of an egg, but a possible crow dropping nearby.'

> '18th May – Fine spring weather. The pair of cranes is now prospecting in the area of a small reed pond half a mile north of the abandoned site. I had prepared a possible nest site on a small island of reed that had been a greylag's nest previously. Observing from a long-established hide I watched the pair of cranes busily adding material to this nest!'

> '21st May – The pair of cranes still not sitting but were dancing on a marsh. They cavorted about, sometimes leaping in the air as much as ten feet upwards with a couple of powerful flaps. One of them would pick up a bit of dead grass and throw it up in the air. They were obviously feeling happy with life. They did not mate at all with this activity, which I expected they might with the new nest arrangements apparently imminent and nearby.'

I shot two foxes in this immediate area within two weeks at about this time.

> '28th May – Crane egg just visible on nest island as I watched a changeover of the pair. Vegetation growing fast and becoming difficult to observe from the hide.'

'3rd June – A different pair of cranes was seen on the grazing marshes only half a mile to the south of the now sitting pair. They both have essentially grey bustles, unlike the resident pair whose bustles are very black.'

'4th June – The grey-bustled pair of cranes was seen going to roost half a mile south of the nesting pair, strangely still in the vicinity but not apparently coming nearer to the nesting pair.'

About this time, the male of the nesting pair appeared very lame and limped badly on one leg. I didn't see any fighting or even meeting of the two males but suspect there was some aggression and possible confrontation between them. There seemed to be some problem at this stage with the nesting pair that calmed down but later, when the chicks had hatched, it recurred. The male was limping for a week but then recovered.

'12th June – Cranes still incubating on reed island. The cattle are now feeding on the marshes adjacent to the crane nesting activity.'

Two goldies swimming, 1st July 2008.

I wanted to make sure the initial grazing would shorten the grass and be completed before the cranes hatched and then would use the same area to feed. On 18th June, the cattle were removed to other grazing. I was expecting the cranes to hatch about 24th June. Two more foxes were killed at about this time.

> '30th June – The lame male was still hobbling. The female was observed in the water just off the nest island and often seen bending down after catching insects off the reed edges near the water. I looked hard through the short green reeds and suddenly there was a view of a tiny gold creature swimming by its parent. Then a second 'goldie' just showed as well. Very exciting that they had successfully hatched at last.'

> '9th July – The crane family is doing fine and rapidly increasing their feeding area to include the grazing marshes. Chicks are growing fast and now stand about nine inches tall but still hugely dependent on the parents for food and protection. The parents will individually pick up a worm, insect or pluck at vegetation to collect other insects to give to the chicks.'

Adult with juvenile, 29th July 2008.

On 18th August, the crane family, including twins, was still actively feeding on the grazing marshes.

Another pair in the fen was seen feeding with a single chick, which was almost flying. There is no evidence that the third pair at Horsey nested.

> '9th September – 4 pm. Crane family feeding on the marshes. The parents flew 50 yards and the two young birds began to run and flap to keep up with them.

They are taking their first flying lessons.'

'10th September – These twins were definitely flying and have achieved lift-off. It is again a very late lift-off date in my experience but successful at last.'

There was a fourth pair that initially tried and failed at Hickling, then nested close to Horsey in an area of mixed marsh to the north, from which two young, later reduced to one, were seen on Heigham Holmes. Later this year, the chance to buy an area of marsh here was too good an opportunity to turn down. This extension to the Horsey Estate did not include exactly where this fourth pair nested, so we cannot claim these as 'ours', but it reinforces the feeling of a successful season, with four young cranes joining the growing east Norfolk flock.

In early November, it was reported that a total of 46 cranes had been observed in the marshes south of Stubb Mill. I know that the pair with twins were seen by myself at the same time and were not part of this group of 46: in other words there were 50 cranes in Broadland. The bigger picture was equally encouraging: by now there were between 11 and 18 nesting pairs in the UK, and though the two pairs at Lakenheath Fen failed to fledge any young for a second year, a pair in Yorkshire was again successful.

Adult with fledged juvenile, 23rd November 2008.

2009
Three pairs of cranes at Horsey raised three chicks.

The UK Crane Working Group met at Horsey Hall in April. The increase and spread of cranes in the Broads had already prompted the formation of an informal working group of conservation-ists here, and this forum was now expanded and formalised to help the exchange of information, including with 'The Great Crane Project' as far west as Somerset.

It was another successful year, but not for the cranes that I followed closely. There were two pairs of cranes in the fen area which, being difficult to get to and watch without disturbance, I left to their own devices as usual, while I concentrated on observing the pair in a more open area to the south.

> '4th May. The resident pair of cranes has built a nest in an unusually open site in the reed pond. By observation from the nearby hide, full incubation has not yet begun. I wanted to check if any eggs had been laid yet. While both adults were absent and feeding together on grazing marshes I was able to observe the nest from an established hide and could just see a single egg. This nest looks somewhat inadequate with the water line nearly flooding its base.'

That evening a pair was observed prospecting for a new nest site half a mile farther south and seems to have abandoned the nest, plus egg, that I had observed earlier.

> '5th May – Cool and drizzle at times, northwest breeze. The pair of cranes is back at the reed pond but the female is working at nest building on a different island, 50 yards to the south of the original nest where the unattended egg was still visible from the hide.'

The female was building up a nest on this small reed island that I had upgraded from an old greylag's nest, from which the brood had hatched and gone a month before. She was poking about at the nest and sometimes sitting down on it, as if to lay.

> 'The male was nearby but I heard no calling between them. I still think it is strange they had left an apparently perfect egg on the other nest site 50 yards away. Perhaps they shared my views that the first nest site was inadequate and too near the water line. What a waste!'

By 15th May, the nesting pair was doing fine at the new site. Both adults were taking time off to feed on the adjacent marshes, but now always one at a time indicating an egg, or two, in the nest.

I could drive my vehicle to within 50 yards of the regular feeding place and watch them as they slowly strut away. My routine was to get out of the vehicle and chuck some barley among the short grass and drive back to the hide. The cranes then slowly return to feed. They seem to take about a crop-full, taking half an hour to feed, then walk away and fly off directly to the nest site on the reed pond. They take a long time to change over on the nest, sometimes 20 minutes.

Ten days after my calculations of the cranes' hatching date had passed they still had shown no signs of hatching. From further observations from the nearby hide, it became apparent that something had gone wrong. The cranes moved away and changed their routine completely and seemed to forget any attachment to both the reed pond and the adjacent grazing marsh feeding area. In June, the RSPB's Film Unit came to film in this area. I was particularly careful that any film operation would not upset the birds, and of course the filming team, led by Nick Upton, was equally cautious. This pair's failure was a big disappointment to the film unit, but no human disturbance had affected the outcome. I visited the nest ten days after the cranes had left it and found one cold and muddy egg.

Elsewhere, out of sight in the fen, two pairs nested successfully. The pair to the south reared one fledgling and half a mile to the north, the regular pair of cranes nested successfully, producing twin fledglings.

2010
Three pairs of cranes at Horsey raised at least one chick.

By mid-April, a pair of cranes was building a nest in the open half of the half acre reed pond, where last year this pair had failed to nest successfully. They completed the nest in approximately three days and she began to sit on the nest at the end of April. I could observe the nest from a long established hide at about 60 yards range. I reckoned that the first egg was laid on 1st May.

The male crane was the laziest I can recall. He was not regularly sitting on the nest during his spells of incubating and often came off the eggs and wandered about the pond in a vague way while the female was having time away from the nest to feed. There was a cold, frosty spell around the 3rd to 5th May and I was worried the eggs might have been bare to the elements at times, when the male crane should have been doing his share of the sitting. As this was the same pair that had nested unsuccessfully on this site in 2009, I was concerned that the incubation had been interrupted by the male's lack of activities during his spell of duty.

With a little egret.

The season went on with reasonably good weather and the eggs were due to hatch on about 30th May. I kept a careful vigil on the nest from the hide in the following week and although the female carried out her full share of sitting on the eggs, the male continued to be inconsistent at his duties. At this time there were some natural visitors close to the nest including two or three little egrets that fed sometimes within yards of the cranes' nest. While the female crane was sitting resolutely unbothered most of the time, she did occasionally lose her cool and chase off the invaders. Once a great white egret arrived to feed but she ignored it. Occasionally greylag geese visited the pond but were usually chased off if they were too close. On one occasion I observed a bittern hunting small invertebrates as it stalked along the reed edge 20 yards from the crane nest.

After two weeks beyond the estimated hatching date, I contacted Andrew Stanbury from the RSPB who was in the area on crane research. He obtained a licence to collect the two eggs and have them examined to establish if they were fertile. It was reported back to us that these eggs had been fertile when laid, but the embryos had ceased to develop after approximately the first week of their existence. This was a disappointment but at the same time offered hope for the future of this pair's efforts.

When Andrew approached the nest, the female stalked away from it in a most unusual way. She walked slowly away from the nest across open water with her head held low along the surface, looking right and left behind her at the intruder. She went back after a few hours but did not climb aboard the nest.

The pair remained in the area until the autumn and certainly never attempted to re-nest. By October this pair of cranes was sometimes roosting at night in the same pond so I hope they still feel it is within their territory.

Flying cranes.

We received better news from the fen. There was a single fledgling in the northern area of the fen and a possibly another single reared in the south of the fen. Both these were observations on neighbouring areas with crane families feeding on marshes adjacent to the Horsey reserve fen. Other pairs of cranes nested within three-quarters of a mile of the reed pond site on land neighbouring the Horsey reserve. If the fledgling was Pair B's, as I think is likely, this brings the number of chicks to nine, possibly 11, that they have fledged since 1988. This is all the more notable as this is the sibling pair, showing no signs of problems from inbreeding. There was further good news as a pair at Hickling successfully fledged one young, and all told there were five cranes fledged in the Broads this year.

This summer, my grandchildren were here at Horsey. A party of ten cranes flew across, by now a familiar part of the scene. My youngest granddaughter, age seven, said "Look, there are Papa's cranes flying over." I felt strongly what a marvellous outcome it was that we could enjoy this as a daily sight at our own home, and how lucky we were that cranes had chosen to come here 30 years ago.

* * *

Horsey cranes 2011 – 2013

The first edition of The Norfolk Cranes' Story book tells the Horsey cranes' story until 2010. This adds observations for the next three years, including what was reported to the UK Crane Working Group. John wrote brief accounts for 2011 and 2012 and these are very much his words, though there isn't a field notebook to draw on so sometimes dates and other information are not precise. The information for 2013 is based on what John related before he died in January 2014.

2011

Two pairs of cranes attempted to nest at Horsey, plus a probable pair. No young were fledged: predation by a marsh harrier seen.

One pair nested 50 metres from a nest of marsh harriers, the cranes' nest hidden in reed at least 100 metres from an open water pond. I made observations from an established hide, 200 metres from the nest. The marsh harriers frequently dipped over the cranes' nest, causing the crane incubating at the time to react and make a beak-clicking noise, a normal reaction to this harassment.

This was the fifth season this pair of cranes had laid eggs. They had always failed to hatch in the past because the male bird rarely took a turn at incubating. In previous seasons, the eggs were frosted by cold spells during the incubation process because he was so lazy about his duties, rarely taking over from the female when she left the nest to feed.

This season there was no frost in May and from my observations from the hide the eggs hatched on or near to 28th May. The adult cranes moved from the nest site hidden in the reeds towards the nearest open water.

However, the eggs of the marsh harriers hatched at about the same date, only 60 metres from the cranes' nest. I saw the male harrier carrying a very small 'goldie' crane chick to its nest to feed its own chicks. I could not tell for certain whether the cranes had more than a single hatched chick, but I suspect there was the brood of two chicks. If so, I don't know the fate of the second chick, but it certainly didn't grow to a size to be visible from the hide.

2012

Three pairs of cranes attempted to nest at Horsey (two confirmed, a third probable) and a fourth pair courted until April, before moving away. Four fledged.

The same pair of cranes as in 2011 remained in the vicinity through out the winter and were quite aggressive to any other cranes' presence. In April 2012, this pair began to show signs of nesting activity quite close to the site of the 2011 nest. I was again observing from the permanent hide 200 metres away. It was most disconcerting to also see that the same pair of marsh harriers was again nesting within 50 metres. So I was pessimistic about any success for the cranes this season as a repeat of last year seemed almost inevitable.

Again, observing from some distance, there was a definite sign that the cranes had hatched in late April. This time the adults moved farther north after I'd seen the signs of hatching, presumably with their chicks, though they couldn't be seen at this stage, to a much safer site at least 400 metres away. They quickly established a new night roost at another pond in a reed marsh where cranes had successfully fledged young in past years. Doing this, they were able to avoid problem of the predatory marsh harriers.

Having previously considered this male crane to be a hopeless parent, I observed that he had become utterly transformed. Throughout the next three months or ten weeks both parent birds were model, attentive parents to twin chicks.

I made frequent visits to hides in sight of the crane family. At first this was to overlook the night roost platform when the twins were growing rapidly, and subsequently to watch the whole family as they fed daily on the adjacent grazing marshes. Neither parent was ever observed leaving the growing twins until 'final lift off' – successful fledging – in mid-July 2012. At last I have reconsidered my opinion of this male crane's ability, but why had it taken six years for him to acquire the conscientious instincts that are needed to be a successful parent remains a mystery.

Another pair of cranes was seen courting in a new area east of the Horsey to Somerton road. The activity ceased after April 2012, for no apparent reason. Two other pairs of cranes attempted nesting in the fen in April 2012 but gave up, possibly after marsh harrier disturbance and/or sedge cutting by human error in the wrong place at the wrong time. Steps have been taken so this should not happen again on the Horsey Estate.

November 2012. There had been infrequent sightings of pair of cranes that had successfully fledged twins throughout the autumn of 2012. On the 18th November (a co-ordinated crane count date organised by the UK Crane Working Group), at noon I observed the family of four birds feeding on the grazing marshes, some 300 metres south of the permanent hide.

The male was intermittently calling a rather pleading shout. I answered his call with my shout of "Grus grus, come and get it!" and, with him in the lead, the family began to walk quite purposefully towards the feeding site. When only at 70 metres distance from me and a mere 40 metres from the food, the family decided this was too close for comfort and gently stretched out their necks and took off, flying towards the north-west and eventually out of my site and into the distance. However, they were back the next day and definitely feeding on the offerings I had put out for them. I shall be able to help the family of four to cope with whatever the 2012/13 winter brings for us.

2013

Two confirmed pairs of cranes at Horsey and probably two more. One pair walked off the estate with two young, one of which survived, and a third fledged bird may have come from a 'probable' pair at Horsey.

John did not write an account for the Horsey cranes for 2013; the above summarises what he reported. The pair of cranes that walked off the Horsey Estate with two chicks went to Heigham Holmes, but one of the twins is believed to have been lost post-fledging. That is unusual: losses to eggs and young before they fledge are commonplace, but it is rare for young birds to fail to survive one they can fly. There were probably an additional two pairs of cranes nesting in the fen. This area is difficult to access and, as in other recent years, they were left to their own devices. An extra fledged bird seen later probably came from one of these pairs, though this is conjecture.

Elsewhere in the Broads there were five confirmed pairs. Four of these failed and a pair at Heigham Holmes fledged one at their second attempt.

Bridget Buxton and Daniel van de Bulk recalled, in February 2014, how the main pair of cranes that John followed seemed to recognise John's voice and his car, a Subaru, and associate these with food. In that vehicle it was easy to approach them closely, but not so in any other.

Part Two
Cranes: History, Observations and Management

Chris Durdin and John Buxton

Chapter 7
Cranes in the UK – a brief history

When cranes first started being seen year-round at Horsey and people in the bird world were talking about the possibility of them nesting, there was doubt in some quarters that they were all wild in origin. The increase in numbers and expansion westwards of the range of cranes was little known in the 1970s, so while that doubt may now seem surprising, at the time it was understandable. There was no folk memory of cranes as a British breeding bird, hardly surprising as they may not have bred since the 17th century, and even then information is sketchy.

There is good historical evidence that cranes used to occur in reasonable numbers in the UK, even though the number that bred is less clear. Place names and documents about feasts suggest hundreds or even thousands of cranes until at least the late Middle Ages.

Boisseau and Yalden, writing in the journal *Ibis*, have gathered place-name, archaeological and documentary evidence for cranes in England. Nearly 300 places include Cran, Carn or Tran, similar to today's Swedish name of *trana* or the German *kranich* and thought to be adapted from Old Norse or Anglo-Saxon names for crane. According to Boisseau and Yalden, no other wild bird appears in so many place-names. Many of these could have been stopping off or wintering areas, so do not prove cranes were breeding. In some cases, grey herons may have been called cranes; even today, people confuse the two species. Place names may be derived for other reasons, such as people called Crane.

However, none of these place names are in the Broads. There are two in Norfolk: Cranworth, south of Dereham, and Cranwich, near Brandon, in the western part of the Brecks. Cranwich, 'the bog where cranes breed' is just eight miles from Lakenheath Fen where cranes have been attempting to breed since 2007. Perhaps the most apposite place name in eastern England is Cranwell, 'the spring where Cranes are found', in Lincolnshire, given that RAF Cranwell is a busy flying training base for the Royal Air Force, though modern fears of bird-strike could make the return of cranes there unwelcome. Boisseau and Yalden found that crane bones are also quite common in archaeological sites, mainly in southern and eastern counties.

Illustrations in manuscripts and records of large numbers of cranes being served at feasts provide further evidence and draw distinctions between cranes and herons. For his Christmas dinner in 1251, Henry III (and presumably others too!) consumed 115 cranes, along with 430 red deer, 200 fallow deer, 200 roe deer, 200 wild swine, 1300 hares, 450 rabbits, 2100 partridges, 290 pheasants, 395 swans, tame pigs, pork brawns, hens, peafowl, salmon and lampreys. Information on what cranes taste like is harder to come by!

There is a lack of information from Scotland and Wales but this reflects, according to Boisseau and Yalden, poorer knowledge about their languages and the lack of sources about place names. Cranes were recorded as being abundant in Ireland, with numerous remains found in lake dwellings and caves, until they were hunted to extinction in the Middle Ages.

Southwell, writing in 1901, and quoted in *The Birds of Norfolk* (Taylor *et al*), was convinced that an ancient record from the Norwich Corporation of a payment for a 'young Pyper crane' proved breeding at Hickling, close to Horsey, in 1543. That apart, there is no direct evidence that cranes bred in Norfolk before the 20th century. Henry Stevenson, in his 'The Birds Of Norfolk' (1870) reviews what was published in 1548 by William Turner, who was educated and lived for 15 years in Cambridge, saying, "it seems not unlikely that his personal acquaintance with the 'pipers' or young cranes was made in the fens of that county". As the then vast Fens stretched into large parts of what are now neighbouring Lincolnshire, Norfolk and Suffolk, it would be surprising if cranes did not also nest in there, and likewise in the Broads and in river valleys through much of lowland England at least, though probably in low densities.

References to cranes shot on the L'Estrange (now Le Strange) Estate at Hunstanton, Norfolk between 1519 and 1533, and of cranes on Christmas menus, point to migrants. Whether the birds that feature in feasts were residents or migrants, their preference for walking away from danger and being a large target once they fly would make them fairly easy to kill with a gun, bow and arrow, cross-bow or even a sling in earlier years, and especially vulnerable on or near a nest. It's easy to imagine hunting taking a heavy toll, and there can be no doubt that large-scale drainage of the Fens and other wetlands would have wiped out large areas of suitable habitats and reduced the prospect of re-colonisation.

Chapter 8
Crane Country: how the Horsey area was shaped

Aerial view of Horsey Mere and marshes looking ENE out to sea. It shows how the Mere's shape is like a mirror image of Africa. Horsey Hall is hidden from view in the trees beyond the Mere, and Horsey Mill is on the right.

Three large rivers, the Bure, Yare and Waveney, run through the great wetland complex of Broadland. The Thurne and Ant rivers are two major tributaries of these, both running roughly from north to south into the River Bure. The River Thurne, Norfolk's shortest river at just five miles, is the closer of the two to the sea.

While there are areas of reedbed and fen in several river valleys, the Upper Thurne has the largest area of near-continuous open fen in Broadland. The area has a relatively low proportion of woodland in comparison with other river valleys, probably due to a combination of the influence of brackish water and its management. This mix of grazing marsh, arable, reedbed and sedge fen must look good to a crane arriving from the North Sea or moving along the coast, with a low human population adding a feeling of security.

The Broads area, as we now know it, was a large estuary until Roman times, open to the sea where Great Yarmouth is now and probably also in the Horsey-Waxham area, which in those days would have been unsuitable for breeding cranes due to a lack of freshwater wetlands. A bar of sand and shingle formed where the town of Great Yarmouth was later built; and by 1500AD, only Breydon Water to its west remained as estuary, as it is today. Layers of saline clay were buried under peat as the sea retreated and vegetation accumulated.

Horsey Mere.

It was not until the 1960s that research by Dr Joyce Lambert and others showed that the origin of the Broads was not as natural lakes, but rather as flooded areas where peat was dug for fuel in the Middle Ages. In the Upper Thurne, digging for clay may have been equally important in the formation of the Broads. There is a low clay embankment around two-thirds of

Horsey Mere, also extending around the sedge and reed fen of Brayden Marsh, with a similar edge to parts of Martham and Hickling Broads. The clay must have been won from the layer underly-ing the surface peat. This makes it more like an embanked reservoir, into which water from the low level marshes was pumped, so rather different in origin and character than Broads created by digging peat. The Mere has reduced in size by about one quarter since the 19th century, but intervention has prevented the Mere's disappearance under encroaching reed and its roughly triangular shape remains.

It's a curiosity that Horsey Mere is the only one of the dozens of broads in Norfolk and north Suffolk known as a 'mere'. Mere is an old English word; locally there are meres well inland in Breckland and in the Fens, as well as scattered elsewhere in Britain. A mere is defined as a lake that is broad in relation to its depth, though there are exceptions, such as Windermere in the Lake District. Though this description is certainly true for Horsey, which is between one and two metres deep, it is also true of all the Broads. Early maps (the Enclosure map, 1812 and the Tithe map, 1840) have a spelling of *Horsey Meer*. A connection with the Dutch meers (lakes) across the North Sea is likely, given the substantial Dutch population in Norfolk, many engaged in the weaving trade, from the 14th to the 16th centuries.

The broads are plainly major landscape features and are a vital part of the rich wildlife mix of the Upper Thurne. Yet cranes have never nested on the edge of Horsey Mere, here as elsewhere preferring to nest near much smaller water bodies. They will also roost standing in shallow water where, as when they nest, the water offers some protection against predators. Though the Thurne Broads are unimportant for breeding and wintering cranes, compared with the natural, semi-natural and man-made vegetation communities, perhaps they have a role in attracting passage birds, or a navigational role for high-flying migrants. Though it isn't true for everywhere that they gather, in several areas where there are concentrations of migrant or wintering cranes there are also large water bodies that may help to draw them in: for example Lake Hornborga in Sweden, the Champagne lakes in France and, in Spain, Lake Gallocanta in the Aragón region. Perhaps east Norfolk's broads have had a role in bringing in the migrants that then stayed to nest.

There are two key factors that shape the land around the River Thurne: salt and man's activities.

All of the main rivers of Broadland are tidal. The penetration of salt water upstream into the river system is to some extent prevented by fresh water flowing downstream so, in general, broads and rivers farther from the sea are less exposed to salt incursions. Yet the Thurne, despite being well upstream, is brackish throughout its length and Horsey Mere is the most brackish of all the broads. This is due to salt water seeping in through the underground aquifer, rather than any tidal influence. The underlying deposits of saline clay also affect the plant communities that have developed above them. Oxidisation of those clays, exposed when wet grassland near Horsey was changed to deep-drained arable, created bright orange deposits of ochre – ferric hydroxide – that flowed down Waxham Cut into Horsey Mere for much of the second half of the 20th century.

Much of the Horsey area and beyond in the Upper Thurne was flooded by the sea in 1938, though escaped serious harm in the 1953 floods. The impact of sea water on vegetation and its wildlife communities is huge, yet the area recovered from this one-off event. Rising sea levels continue to cast a shadow over the area, though the Environment Agency has pledged to maintain the sea defences from Happisburgh to Winterton for at least 50 years (taken literally,

2048), a stretch of coastline that includes the large sand dunes maintained as a sea wall at Horsey and Waxham.

With respect to man's activities, the pattern of enclosure and land ownership in the area has had an impact on land management that continues today.

For the most part, drainage of the peat floodplain was small scale until the passing of the Enclosure Acts in the 18th and 19th centuries. Many of the present land boundaries and, indeed, current land use came about as a direct result of Parliamentary Enclosure. The Acts took away common rights and kick-started co-operation and management by landowners to drain the peat fens. The Upper Thurne seems to have been distinctive for the grand scale on which Parliamentary Enclosure was carried out. This complete restructuring of the landscape was possible because there were still great tracts of undrained, unenclosed wetland in this area up until the early 19th century and settlement was, and remains, relatively sparse.

Ochre flowing from Waxham Cut into Horsey Mere.

Up until the mid 19th century, the fens of Broadland were still being exploited for a wide variety of fen products such as reed and sedge for roofing and marsh hay. After about 1875, however, the quantities of materials being taken off site began to decline as local demand for fen products fell. By the end of World War II, very few areas of fen vegetation remained under traditional management, or indeed any form of management. Several large, privately-owned Broadland estates, for example at Hickling, Horsey and the Bure Marshes, continued to cut reed and sedge, but the majority of fenland sites fell into disuse. The most obvious outcome of the decline in management was the rapid invasion by scrub into large tracts of fen. Much of the present-day carr woodland on drier ground became established during this period, but much less in the Upper Thurne than in other Broadland river valleys. Though reed and sedge are still harvested at Hickling, Horsey and Martham, the commercial element is now less of a driver than conservation management. With The National Trust and Norfolk Wildlife Trust as major landowners, as well as the Horsey Estate, this looks set to continue for the foreseeable future.

Top: Thatching a house on the Horsey Estate. **Below:** Reed is still harvested at Horsey.

Chapter 9
Observations on cranes

Choice of nest sites

The cranes' preference is to have open water on at least one side, which gives a clear view of the approach of any mammalian predators. The nests are not always on an island, which would give the best protection, but that may be due to a shortage of suitable sites at Horsey. Nests are not normally on the sides of dykes as they would be vulnerable here to foxes moving along the dyke edge. The sole exception was the one nest east of the Horsey-Somerton road, in 1989, which was in a narrow strip of reed between two ditches, but was deserted probably owing to disturbance from cattle.

Since Chinese water deer became established they have produced paths through the reeds, paths that can easily be followed by a fox. Naturally no choice of nest site can protect the eggs and young from aerial predators such as harriers, bitterns or crows.

A cut strip makes it easier for cranes to walk from their nest to feeding areas.

Cranes also nest in thick saw-sedge, though this makes moving in and out of the nest area a challenge for the young. No nest has ever been on the edge of Horsey Mere: they are tucked away out of sight in smaller ponds in the fen or reed.

Because much of the feeding in spring and summer takes place on grazing marshes, nests are always within striking distance of these. Usually they are some 200-300 yards from a grazing marsh, but they may be up to half a mile. At Horsey, the Estate often cuts a wide track, well ahead of the breeding season, from potential nesting areas to the grazing marshes. This makes it easier for the cranes to walk through the vegetation along an open roadway from the nesting site to feeding areas in the grazing marshes. Usually, this cut is some 12 feet wide to reduce the risk of a fox ambushing a young crane on a narrow track.

Some areas of adjacent grazing marshes, in recent years, have had electric sheep netting, which bars the way for cranes walking with a youngster. The adult birds now choose to nest away from these fenced areas, apparently in response to the fences.

Camouflage

On several occasions, incubating female cranes have been seen putting muddy water onto their backs, causing the feathers to go brown. Turning grassland to deep-drained arable on the Thurne upstream from Horsey creates deposits of orange ochre; this is ferric hydroxide, released from soils once flooded by saline water, and has affected Horsey Mere for five decades. The colour of ochre means the effect of this on plumage is quite marked and reasonably obvious if the light is good as it is on the area exposed to view from above. It is a sure sign that they have started incubation.

> "I have never experienced any other bird which voluntarily carries out this camouflage technique. How have they learnt to do this? Has instinct taught them or is it proof of a very clever bird?" JJB

Incubation

Incubation of the eggs is between 28 and 31 days, typically 30 days. It is possible to judge when incubation has started when a single crane is at the feeding grounds for the first time, rather than the pair feeding together.

Both sexes share incubation, usually sitting for between 90 minutes and two hours before a changeover. In 1983, warden Sandra Anderson observed and recorded this in detail. Careful watching of the second nest of Pair A, daily for 14 hours, allowed information on the length of incubation shifts by the parents to be collected. Forty-nine counts of sitting times were logged, varying between 21 and 234 minutes, with an average of 102 minutes. Both male and female incubated, but it was not possible to tell if there was any difference between the lengths of incubation, as it was difficult to distinguish between them in flight as they came into or left the nest.

Some pairs share incubation fairly equally, though the female always broods on the nest overnight while the male stands on one leg a few feet away, usually in water. In some cases the male fails in his duties and does not incubate when his turn comes, leaving the female to do the bulk of the incubation. These pairs seem more likely to fail.

Common cranes incubate as soon as the first of the two eggs is laid. The interval between egg-laying is two days, rarely one or three. This is true of all cranes of the sub-family Gruinae ('typical cranes') including the genus *Grus*. By contrast, crowned cranes, sub-family Balearicinae, incubate when the clutch of two eggs is complete. It is curious that cranes (and great bustards, to which cranes are only distantly related) should hatch young asynchronously. It is known that raptors and owls do this to adjust to variable food supplies in any year. In broods of bird of prey, Cainism occurs regularly, the killing of a younger sibling by an older nest mate, but there has been no observation or evidence of this in cranes at Horsey.

Cranes prefer to have open water on at least one side of their nest so they can see approaching predators.

Fledging success

During 30 years at Horsey (1981-2010), 67 attempts at breeding have produced between 18 and 21 young. This gives an average productivity of between 27% and 31% – less than one chick fledged for every three crane pairs attempting to nest. Fledging two young successfully remains the exception here, confirmed just four times in these 67 nesting attempts.

By contrast, though our information set is incomplete, fledging success has been higher away from Horsey, including two young fledged at least six times in about 34 nesting attempts in ten years between 2001 and 2010. Pair D has successfully produced twins at least four times in three locations, including Horsey, so it may be partly due to their parental skills and also to the variety of nest sites. It seems likely that moving reduces the chances of predators such as foxes finding the nest or vulnerable chicks.

There is nothing to show that food supply is a constraint on the number of young cranes fledged at Horsey. Experience and predation are certainly factors. Young pairs seem invariably to fail at the first attempt. Otherwise, we think that predation is the most consistent influence on cranes' fledging success.

Roosting platforms

How and where cranes build nests have been well observed and recorded by crane watchers in Europe. However, building a roosting platform, a piece of behaviour observed at Horsey, appears not to have been recorded elsewhere – certainly it is not in *The Birds of the Western Palearctic*. We therefore describe this in some detail.

Creating a roosting platform, in addition to the nest for laying eggs, was first recorded at Horsey in 1997. This was in the reedbed area close to where they nest: this behaviour has not been seen in the saw-sedge nesting area. Building a platform of reeds on which to roost overnight, in addition to a nest platform, is now a regular part of chick rearing at Horsey. They roost on the 'egg nest' for about a week after hatching, but then move to the roost platform.

Left: Night roost: a chick climbs on the female's back.
Below: Walking towards the night roost, 28th June 2005.

This is how it is recorded in the Estate's notebooks for 12th May 1997.

> 'They have twice retired for the night back to the nest on the edge of the uncut area. The young reed colt [reeds roughly between and 18 and 24 inches high] is growing very fast at present and is about two foot tall i.e. up to halfway covering the view of an adult crane. The adult pair each evening at the 'going to bed stage' were busily building a nest platform from whatever material is to hand.'

‘I filmed some of this activity from the hide at about 50 yards range. The male kept picking up little bits of wet reed and grass and chucking it vaguely in the direction of the female beside him. She was methodically treading down the nest platform as she slowly turned a complete circle, step by step with her head down out of my sight. She eventually subsided onto the bed for the night.’

‘What a nasty wet bed to roost upon although her warmth must be a comfort.’

The roosting platform is placed on a rushy edge to a reedbed on the edge of open water of roughly 3-4 inches in depth. Observations at the night roost revealed that the small chicks at this stage of growth – up to three weeks old – climb aboard through the feathers on the female’s back, sheathed by her wings. The chicks may be completely hidden or their heads can pop up as they look around from their place of comfort. When the young get quite big, after about a month, they are no longer tolerated on her back and they roost alongside the adults.

Chicks swim almost as soon as they are hatched.

Swimming

Chicks can swim almost as soon as they are hatched, looking rather duck-like as they move away from the nest or across dykes to or within grazing marshes. Most of the places they frequent, including nests, are relatively shallow, up to one foot deep, so easy for an adult crane to wade through. John Buxton has only once seen an adult swimming in more than 25 years. That crane – without young at the time – had to cross a wide dyke, about 12 feet across. It simply swam across. With the neck held low, it looked more like a cormorant than a goose or swan, though with a neck rather straighter than the kink of a cormorant.

Feeding

Cranes are known to be omnivorous with a great range of prey and vegetable matter taken. They are quite a predator, taking frogs and young birds; they have been seen taking avocet chicks on the scrape at Horsey. Not surprisingly, the characteristically aggressive avocets mob cranes and lapwings dive-bomb them, showing that these wading birds are aware of the potential threat to their chicks.

Several times bigger? That doesn't deter an avocet.

The cranes' range of food and how this varies through the year is very apparent. In early spring, as the worms start to move, the cranes start digging, and worms may well be their main food source in spring and summer. The whole neck moves very energetically. The chick is fed on insects, snatched by the adult cranes and fed beak-to-beak to the chick.

John Buxton watched this process one day in 1986.

> "The parent bird caught a dragonfly as it flew past and trotted a few steps to one side. It leant down with the dragonfly in the tip of its beak as a small golden head appeared and grabbed the insect from below."

For adults and growing young, potatoes are a favoured food. Though they are especially valuable as a food source in winter, adults will eat potatoes in the summer too. Wildfowl, especially mallards and the large numbers of greylag geese that moved into the area during the 1980s, are partial to rotten potatoes. Cranes will drive mallards away from the potato pile. They prefer small, healthy potatoes, especially when beginning to sprout, but will break up larger potatoes. Occasionally they will wash any dry, dusty potatoes if there is a puddle or dyke edge handy.

In recent years at Horsey, red deer will eat potatoes left out overnight. One evening, cranes flew away from the potato pile as a single stag moved in to feed, though the cranes would have gone to roost around that time anyway so the deer may not yet be competing directly. In 2004, an electric fence – one strand at waist height – was put around the potato pile to deter deer. It was also seen to put off the cranes, which prefer to walk rather than fly, so was removed after about a month. Now smaller quantities of potatoes are put out daily, in the morning, rather than weekly: time-consuming, but effective.

Grain is provided, here also attracting a jackdaw, a mallard and stock doves.

Other food occasionally provided for cranes at Horsey includes sugar beet, barley, maize and acorns. These last two are also common food sources for the tens of thousands of cranes wintering in Extremadura in central Spain where they feed mainly in maize stubble fields and on the acorns of holm oaks – here *Quercus rotundifolia* rather than *Quercus ilex* – in the extensive areas of wood pasture known locally as *dehesa*.

During winter, cranes also feed in cereal fields. Though they may be taking insects, they also can be seen eating the young cereal shoots, both wheat and barley. During their first winter at Horsey, John Buxton observed one crane pluck the individual seeds off the head of a piece of ryegrass while standing with one foot on the stalk. They also take the seeds from grass and will strip seed heads from wheat.

Between feeding sessions birds may rest, either down on their hocks or standing on one leg. Particularly on hot, sunny days, crane chicks will take a nap by lying down on the grass.

Cranes and livestock

In winter, cranes are happy to be in the same field as cattle or sheep, but families with young prefer to feed on grazing marshes without livestock, which at Horsey means cattle. This may be due to disturbance, for example frolicking youngsters or, as cattle near Horsey are checked daily, avoiding contact with people. But food supply may be the key factor. In spring and summer, both adult and young cranes can be seen picking off invertebrates from ungrazed wetland vegetation. This is consistent with the results of recent studies at RSPB Lakenheath Fen that show ungrazed fen has a larger biomass of invertebrates than grazed fen, so providing a better food supply for cranes.

The grazing season at Horsey runs from the second half of May to October, though cattle are often excluded from marshes on which cranes are likely to rely. The grazing marshes here are cut in the autumn, after the cattle have gone, to reduce the dominance of soft rush *Juncus effusus*, known locally as pin rush.

Whether it is a disadvantage to have any livestock near to breeding cranes is an interesting question. Cranes with small chicks feed at Hickling where there is a low density of livestock, in this case steers. Konik ponies, Highland cattle and even water buffaloes are increasingly used to manage large wetland nature reserves with low intensity grazing to help keep a mosaic of open areas and higher vegetation. In these more extensive, less managed circumstances, it seems likely that there will be a trade-off between the value of livestock in keeping areas open and any reduction in invertebrate food supply.

Sounds of cranes

The commonest sound of cranes is 'unison' trumpeting, though duet is a better description. One bird will start calling, usually the male, and the other of the pair then joins in, or sometimes other birds. Or perhaps 'harmony' is more apt than 'unison': the musical interval is a minor third, the same as that of a cuckoo's song in early spring. This call is often made on or near the nest, and when courting, but also frequently out of the breeding season when crane pairs are feeding or walking around. It seems to be a contact call, acting as reassurance when the other bird joins in.

On seeing a fox, a single alarm call is made, followed by the unison call, be it on the nest or out on the marsh.

A mechanical bill-clattering sound is made in reaction to marsh harriers flying close to a cranes' nest. Whereas a bittern or an avocet will fly up to see off a harrier, the larger, slower, less manoeuvrable crane cannot. On one occasion, the crane and harrier nests were only about 50 yards apart. The crane could not be seen in thick fen vegetation, but the sound of beak-clapping in response to the harrier could still be heard.

Unison trumpeting.

High-flying cranes on migration or otherwise, sound different again, with an evocative *gru gru* bugling call. It's a gentle, joyful call you can hear over great distances: it can take some time to find the specks in the sky. Birds on the ground may call in response to the high-flying birds.

The high-pitched 'peeping' call of a juvenile crane continues while it is dependent on its parents. At the end of the young crane's first winter, the adults chase the bewildered offspring out of the family group. It will then have to fend for itself, joining up with other immature cranes, if there are any in the area. The young crane will be losing its peeping call at this stage: its voice breaks to a croak instead.

This diary entry for 20th March 1989, about Pair B, shows how adult cranes intent on nesting become intolerant of others, even their own offspring, when the nesting season approaches, and that for an immature, peeping is no defence from being chased by parents.

> 'Young pair of cranes chasing off their own young bird of 1988. Quite vicious chase by the male parent and the young one was peeping loudly as it flew over my head quite close. I had been told they chased the young one off when it ceases to peep and the voice breaks to croaking. Apparently, not so.'

Peeping is normally heard from young birds on the ground, though this 1989 account illustrates an exception. The high peeping was heard again from the 1988 youngster as late as 22nd April 1989.

What's in a name?

It's from cranes in flight that we hear their '*gru gru*' sound – from which comes the Latin *grus* and the scientific name of *Grus grus*. Other Latin-based languages are similar. The Spanish *grulla*, the Portuguese *grou*, the French *grue cindrée* and Italian *gru* come from this root. Curiously, in Romanian, another Latin-based language, crane is *cocorul-mare*. The mechanical crane on a building site is sometimes the same word (e.g. French) and sometimes different (e.g. *grúa* in Spanish).

The English name crane is plainly Anglo-Saxon in origin, being more similar to the German *kranich*, Norwegian/Danish *trane* or the Swedish *trana*. These crop up in place names, such as Cranwich and Tranmere.

In Greek, the crane is *γερανός* (geranos) – both bird and machine. Botanists and gardeners will recognise the link with *Geranium*, the large genus of both wild and cultivated cranesbills. The related red and pink pot plant often called geranium is strictly speaking *Pelargonium*, and though closely related to the true geraniums, its name comes from stork (pelargos); *Erodium*, storksbill, evokes the heron (erodios).

Herb Robert *Geranium robertianum*, a common species of cranesbill, grows outside the back door at Horsey Hall. Note the crane-like head on the seedpod.

Crane displays

1) Threat display

A typical threat display is a resident pair responding to an intruder. The pair will make the unison call; the male will raise his bustle, hold his head and beak high and do a stately walk with deliberate, elegant steps towards his rival. He may call and may run after the intruder, at which the intruder will probably fly or walk away. Rarely, the intruder competes by holding his ground.

Another threat display observed at Horsey involves pairs that are nesting close to each other, with a dyke forming a territorial boundary. In this case, the nests were about half a mile apart and the dyke in open grazing marsh appeared to be a mutually agreed boundary in the feeding area. The display involved birds standing some 10 or 12 feet apart across a dyke, calling (bugling) with heads and bustles held high for about 30 seconds, followed by a proud walk away with big steps, still with head held high and bustle partly raised, before being deflated. One male did so much of this territorial jousting that he failed to do his share of incubating on the nest about a quarter of a mile away. This nest failed at the egg stage, though how much the male's distraction caused this is unclear.

The dark patterning on the neck below the red patch may vary, helping us to recognise individual birds. On one bird the black is in a horseshoe shape, on another more like the loop shape on a tennis ball, or it may come to a point.

In winter, threatening behaviour is sometimes seen if there is an intrusion into what a pair regards as still its territory. Birds are then roosting as a loose group, with any family party around 20 yards from non-breeders. Naturally, threat display takes place mostly in the breeding season, with antagonistic behaviour seen from mid-March. This may encourage the dispersal of non-breeding birds, which usually move away from crane territories in early April, though this varies according to the weather.

In the threat posture, the red on the head shows strongly. Typically, the red patch seems quite dark but shows as a vivid red on a displaying male, if seen in good light.

Aerial attack can be part of the threat armoury, witnessed on one occasion. Both birds were in flight: the male of the first pair of cranes at Horsey chased a young male crane away by diving at him, head and beak first, at one point making contact with the immature bird, which flew away.

2) Dancing display

The most famous crane display must be their dancing courtship, though words inadequately describe it. Some of the movement can be at any time of the year; with a group of cranes it can be infectious, one bird setting off movement from others in the group with running, head-bobbing and bows, or marching side by side with stiff legs, like soldiers on parade. All of these movements can be thrown into the mix in spring, when dancing happens most often and with greatest excitement. It starts with two standing birds with head and neck held low, beak pointed forwards, wings and bustle at least partly raised. Then a little run, perhaps two to five paces, and they throw themselves into the air with one powerful flap. At any time of year, display will often end with a little shake and feeding resumes.

Every year is leap year for cranes.

3) Mating display

Typically there is some dancing before mating and reversed mounting, with the female leaping on the male, which seems to happen at Horsey before mating, as if the female is giving encouragement. Before mating, the male raises his bustle into a fan, the female walks in front, stretching out her wings and leaning forwards. The male then mounts, balancing on his tarsi (lower legs), the female leaning forwards to be horizontal. The actual copulation takes three or four seconds. The male then jumps over the head of the female, landing and running a few paces. They then both run around, shake, preen; they may bob heads together, off and on, for a minute or more. The male's bustle goes down and feeding continues. Immediately before and during copulation there can be some calling, a quiet 'graw graw graw', accelerating to a gentle but excited 'grik grik grik grik', but pinpointing whether these come from the male or female is difficult from a distance.

Mating cranes at Horsey, 9th April 2008.

Migration 'spiral'

During sunny weather in late winter or early spring, a distant croak may alert one to high-flying cranes. At least a pair and sometimes up to ten cranes have been seen slowly flying higher, some criss-crossing in the sky. Sometimes this may prompt other birds on the ground, including immature birds, to join the group. In common with other crane species, take-off is into the wind, first leaning forwards to get some idea of wind strength, flapping hard to get aloft, then spiralling upwards. Though it is tempting to think that bright weather prompts thoughts of migration, it may simply be that sunshine is needed to create good thermals for effortless soaring. Though the Horsey cranes have travelled widely within the UK and incoming migrants have boosted their numbers, there is no evidence of any having migrated or moved abroad.

Handover signal

The handover routine between adult cranes on the nest or with young provokes a fascinating display flight. It happens at varying heights, as high as a few hundred yards, and may also happen when other cranes fly over, suggesting it is a signal establishing territory.

The incoming bird's flight includes a hesitant, delayed flap of the primaries. At the end of the down stroke, the incoming bird, at about 20 feet, holds its wings well forward and holds its wing tips there, the primaries angled down, with a clear delay before the upwards flap. Curiously, lapwings do something similar. This only seems to happen when cranes have eggs or young. Both sexes do it, though it is more common in the male.

Chapter 10
Conservation management at Horsey

An 'Area of Special Protection'

Under the Bird Protection Acts of 1954 and 1967, there was a now rather quaint-sounding provision for 'bird sanctuaries'. This can prohibit entry except by permission – as it does at Horsey – and confers extra protection for birds within the defined areas. In summary, special penalties apply to those entering these areas without permission, killing or taking wild birds or their eggs, or disturbing nest-building or dependent young. The list of 31 'bird sanctuaries' was for many years found at the back of the RSPB's publication *Wild Birds and the Law* but is otherwise little known or mentioned. Sites include Cley Marshes in Norfolk and Hornsea Mere in Yorkshire – the latter sometimes a source of confusion with Horsey Mere.

Under the Wildlife and Countryside Act of 1981, this provision was retained, but re-named an 'Area of Special Protection' (AoSP). While sounding more modern, this actually adds to the confusion as it sounds very much like a Special Protection Area (SPA). An SPA is rather different, being an internationally important site for birds designated under the EU's Birds Directive. The Horsey-Hickling area is also part of the Upper Thurne Broads and Marshes SPA and Ramsar site, the latter shorthand for internationally important wetlands recognised under the Ramsar Convention that was adopted in the Iranian city of Ramsar in 1971 and came into force in 1975. The area is also a Site of Special Scientific Interest (SSSI).

Horsey is one of just three AoSPs declared since the 1981 Act. Dr Martin George, then Regional Officer for English Nature and an influential figure in conservation in the Broads over several decades, suggested at the Hickling Committee that an AoSP be considered for Hickling nature reserve to help safeguard its nesting harriers. This was quickly ruled out due to access needs there for Norfolk Wildlife Trust members, but seemed to be potentially valuable for the more private Horsey Estate.

A proposal was drawn up for an AoSP covering the estate's marshes west and south of Horsey Mere, though excluding the Mere due to navigation rights. Though these navigation rights remain year-round, to reduce disturbance to wintering waterfowl, boats are requested not to enter Horsey Mere during the winter, from 1st November to 1st March.

While cranes were the immediate reason that prompted this process, nesting bitterns and marsh harriers and the winter roost of harriers added weight to the idea. Following two years of consultations, including with neighbours, North Norfolk District Council and Horsey Parish Council, the AoSP came into force on 17th March 1988 (Order no. 324 from the Department of Environment).

The bitterns, marsh harriers and bearded tits nesting at Horsey are on Schedule 1 of the Wildlife and Countryside Act, which gives them a higher degree of protection during the breeding season and, prior to recent changes in the law, allowed courts to impose higher penalties. Cranes are not on Schedule 1, so they and their nests and eggs have the same level of protection as, say, a blackbird or a robin. For crane to be added to Schedule 1 would have been a pretty strong indication that cranes were nesting somewhere in the UK, which at that time was best avoided. The AoSP was a way of conferring that special protection on cranes, as well as restrictions on access.

Nonetheless, cranes are plainly rare and vulnerable as a nesting bird and should be on Schedule 1, especially now that they nest away from the Horsey area. The RSPB has proposed that this obvious anomaly (and some others) should be rectified, but the lack of progress seems to be due to the absence of a routine system for Government to update these lists.

Nearly all the nests at Horsey have been within the AoSP. The exceptions were the one nest east of the Somerton-Horsey road and several nests over the years on land owned by the Norfolk Wildlife Trust immediately adjacent to the Horsey AoSP.

The most serious security alert was in April 1994. John Buxton was in a hide keeping an eye on the cranes and could see a human face looking out of another hide about 400 yards away. He contacted the police and then organised an ambush on what turned out to be two people. By this time, one man was climbing over the fence that had a notice saying 'No access', along with the details of the Area of Special Protection. The other man was on the safe side of the fence. John was worried, as they could have seen bitterns, marsh harriers and cranes moving into their nest sites.

To help prepare the prosecution case, the Crown Prosecution Service solicitor, Kevin Eastwick, visited Horsey with RSPB Investigations staff. To see the lie of the land, this included a trip by boat to visit the hide from where the incident had been observed.

The people involved were known to the RSPB, having been seen in suspicious circumstances near nests of rare birds, including eagles in Scotland. Perhaps they were doing a 'recce' to provide information for egg-collectors? The case came before Great Yarmouth Magistrates and resulted in a fine of £500, plus £75 costs.

Joan Childs from the RSPB's Investigations team was in court, and dealt with the inevitable news interest afterwards. Her notes record:

> 'John left in case there was any media, and asked me to cover for him – tricky as we can't mention the cranes. He said he felt very unchivalrous but I told him that was my job.'

Later that year, on 8th May, the cranes moved from their nest for unexplained reasons. John suspects that collectors took the eggs, though there is no proof or knowledge of cranes' eggs appearing in egg collections. This was the only case where people were suspected of disrupting the cranes.

Grazing marsh management

Livestock, cattle especially, are vital for maintaining the grazing marshes on which cranes like to feed. Much of the grazing marsh at Horsey in managed under prescriptions set by tier 3 of the Broads Environmentally Sensitive Area (ESA). This allows grazing from 15th May, a date originally set to minimise trampling of the nests of breeding waders like lapwings and redshanks. In practice, it is easy to start grazing a little later than this on fields near cranes' nests, where they are most likely to feed.

There is no doubt that the Horsey Estate would have struggled financially without the support of the ESA system for the wildlife-friendly management of grazing marshes. The Estate is optimistic that this should continue when the ten-year ESA agreement ends and is replaced by the new Environmental Stewardship scheme. Management then should be more objective-led, rather than following management prescriptions, which should work just as well.

Redshank.

Predator control at Horsey

No adult crane has ever been taken by a predator at Horsey, so far as we know. Foxes are highly likely to be responsible for the loss of several young cranes at Horsey and probably eggs too, but this is, most of the time, hard to prove. Foxes may well have put off nesting or incubating cranes too. As noted earlier, tracks left by Chinese water deer make it easy for foxes to move through reeds or fen.

One particular incident, in 1977, comes to mind in relation to foxes and cranes. A fox was following two crane chicks, twins with parents, at some distance. John Buxton was in a hide, and they were working slowly up-wind in his direction, though at first he could not see the fox. The male crane kept looking back. The cranes passed his position some 40 yards away, then moved on about 100 yards past him, when he saw the fox coming up about 200 yards behind the cranes. John had a rifle in the hide and waited until the fox was within range and shot it, cleanly killing it with one shot. He was worried that the shot might frighten the cranes. However, the male crane ran across about 100 yards to where the dead fox was lying. The crane looked at the dead fox quite closely, took off and flew back to the family and when it landed it appeared to be 'happy' because its bustle went down, having been up, as if to say to the rest of the family that the problem had gone. It was extraordinary that the cranes did not panic when they heard the shot and equally strange that the male should return to the fox's corpse.

A few foxes are shot each year at Horsey. More are shot on the neighbouring estate to the south, which employs a full-time gamekeeper.

Plainly young chicks are especially vulnerable, but in the period 1st – 10th August 2006 two large young cranes also disappeared, probably due to fox predation. The two birds, from the same nest, were about eight and a half weeks old, so at a stage at which one might expect they would be safe.

Swallowtail
Swallowtail butterflies are arguably as distinctive and special to the Broads as cranes. Milk parsley, the food plant for swallowtail caterpillars, is common in the fen areas at Horsey. Cut fen encourages ragged robin (pictured) and the butterflies seem especially to be attracted to pink flowers such as this and hemp agrimony, but they also favour pink wallflowers in the garden at Horsey Hall, about a quarter of a mile from the marshes.

Carrion crows and magpies are actively live-trapped on the Horsey Estate in spring, as eggs are imminent or in nests. This is to help safeguard ground-nesting birds on the estate, especially lapwings, though magpies have not been seen attacking a young crane or taking eggs. Trapping is done with a Larsen trap, as on many estates, and as recommended by the Game Conservancy Trust. A Larsen trap is made of wire on a wood frame, inside which a live crow or magpie is kept as a lure, plus a supply of food and water. The curious crow or magpie lands on the top of the trap and falls inside through a swing trap-door. The Larsen trap is regularly inspected and the trapped bird humanely despatched. About 25-30 of both crows and magpies are caught this way each spring. Trapping of crows and magpies stops before cranes lay any later clutches, often those from which young are fledged, and this does not seem to create a problem.

Jackdaws sometimes come on the marshes but are not a worry. Rooks are common, often searching for leatherjackets – crane fly larvae – and might, in theory, be a problem, but there has been no known case of rooks taking cranes' eggs at Horsey.

Marsh harriers often nest quite close to cranes in the marsh. They will swoop over cranes' nests, provoking a mechanical clacking from the bird on the nest. The most vulnerable stage would be when the two young cranes are up to about ten days old, when it is difficult for the adult birds to protect both youngsters. Predation by marsh harriers has never been observed, but it could account for losses at this stage.

An avocet mobs a marsh harrier.

Chapter 11
What future for cranes in Britain?

Cranes seem to be well established in the UK now, or rather re-established, given that they were once a fairly widespread breeding bird, albeit probably never very common. Over three decades since the cranes' arrival in 1979, they have increased to a UK population in 2010 of a minimum of 13 nesting pairs, including at least eight pairs in the Broads. In addition there are other non-breeding or unconfirmed pairs in the Broads and elsewhere and a winter flock in Broadland numbering 50 or more individuals.

It's a very solid foothold in the UK, but could hardly be described as a rapid growth in numbers. Looking back on the early years, the authors could have imagined – and indeed feared – that one or two deaths in the small Horsey group could have stopped their progress for the foreseeable future. The fact that that didn't happen is partly because the Horsey area proved so ideal for both breeding and wintering cranes, boosted by a big effort to help them in all seasons. But it was and is even more down to the cranes' own ability to survive. Their remarkable longevity means that though breeding failures are common, once they get to the flying stage then each bird is likely to survive for many years, even decades. It may take five years before they attempt to nest, and in the first couple of years inexperienced birds usually fail, but over the following years they seem to succeed in not only replacing themselves but also putting new birds into the British population.

The Horsey birds were originally migrants and immigration continues to help. As well as home-grown cranes, the small but growing group at Horsey has been regularly boosted by additional migrating birds that were probably drawn to stay by the resident group. The growth in crane numbers elsewhere in Europe and especially their westward spread will accelerate this process. Migrants pass through the UK every year, and the more birds there are breeding and migrating closer to the UK, the more often we will witness an invasion such as happened in 2007. That influx was probably the source of the two pairs now at Lakenheath Fen in Suffolk, which are starting to fledge young and top up the local population. Migrant birds have the further bonus that they bring in fresh genes, reducing any risk of a small UK population suffering problems from inbreeding through a limited gene pool.

Captive breeding and release looks likely to increase numbers further. There are free-flying birds that originate from Pensthorpe Waterfowl Park in Norfolk, including one paired with a wild bird. These are accidental releases, but work is under way in the West Country on a bigger scale. The Great Crane Project released 21 cranes on the Somerset Levels and Moors in September 2010, hatched from eggs taken from a wild population of cranes in Germany, the Schorfheide-

Chorin Biosphere reserve, Brandenburg. From a Horsey perspective, we were initially concerned that somewhere in East Anglia might be selected for this project, confusing the natural population growth that already had a good head of steam. To be fair to the project partners this was never the plan, with the release site in Somerset, well away from eastern England, selected after a rigorous appraisal process. Views on this idea vary. On the one hand, it can be argued that cranes are now back for good, and that it's only a question of time before they spread to suitable habitats throughout the UK, be that from locally produced birds or migrants. On that basis, the expense of a captive breeding project would be better off put into conservation projects elsewhere. On the other hand, it took three decades from the initial re-colonisation for the number of pairs to reach double figures, and very few people get the pleasure of seeing cranes without actively seeking them in east Norfolk. Cranes can be symbolic of great wetlands and could be used as a flagship species to justify major wetland restoration on the Somerset Levels and Moors, which will benefit a large range of wildlife.

Every conservationist will be in favour of wetland creation, whether or not cranes are the peg on which to hang the idea. Undoubtedly cranes use big wetlands and Lakenheath Fen shows that newly created wetlands will attract them. It has been an article of faith throughout the Horsey project that the size and mix of the fens, grazing marshes and pools in the Horsey-Hickling area have been what has driven cranes' success here. Large wetlands are also much less likely to be disturbed by people, and the size and private nature of the Horsey Estate have kept disturbance of cranes by people to a minimum.

While large fens or reedbeds and lack of disturbance help, it may not be as essential as we first thought, or it may have become less crucial. Denmark now has about 120 pairs of cranes, many of which nest in small wetlands, with birds feeding on nearby grassland or arable. In 2006, a pair of cranes nested at the Norfolk Wildlife Trust's Hickling Broad nature reserve by the Weavers' Way long distance footpath (albeit for a period quickly closed off) and within easy viewing range of a public hide. The eggs from this pair were not lost to disturbance by people, rather to a fox that was seen, from the hide, taking the eggs. This all suggests that although large, undisturbed wetlands are the best habitat for cranes, as numbers grow they are bound to nest in less ideal habitats, though perhaps with a reduced level of success.

Predators will also have a big influence. Man as a predator was the critical reason that caused cranes to become extinct in the UK, alongside habitat loss. It seems reasonable to assume that the days of cranes featuring in state banquets are over. Legal protection has not eliminated egg collecting in the UK, but it would be surprising if it reached a level that threatened the crane population.

The experience at Horsey is that the adults survive well but eggs and chicks are very vulnerable to predators. Though there are many potential predators of crane eggs and chicks, including crows, marsh harriers and bitterns, foxes have been by far the biggest problem. Their impact has been reduced at Horsey, even if not entirely eliminated, by a regular programme of predator control – namely shooting foxes. Many big nature reserves have a fox control programme from which cranes will benefit. But fox control is time-consuming and expensive and there are mixed views about it, coupled with public relations challenges. With the population of foxes at an historically high level they will be a threat to cranes even on the best-managed reserves. As cranes spread into more peripheral nesting sites, so the losses to foxes will increase.

A winter flock of 14 cranes, December 2006.

But we are already at a point where a combination of locally fledged birds and migrants is driving a steady growth in numbers, and the best guess is that predators and disturbance will slow rather than stop this existing trend. There must be a good prospect of cranes colonising lowland wetlands throughout England and Wales, and even returning to Ireland. Given that there are tens of thousands of pairs of cranes in Scandinavia and eastern Europe, many nesting in or by small pools in peat bogs tucked away in coniferous forests, it seems likely that the occasional attempts to nest in Scotland will increase, more an offshoot of the Scandinavian population than an expansion of the East Anglian group.

The impact of climate change is another factor to weigh. Though the wintering flocks in Extremadura in Spain remain, still numbering around 100,000 birds, increasingly cranes also overwinter in their traditional migration refuges in northeast France. The best-known area is Lac du Der-Chantecoq in the Champagne-Ardenne region, where traditionally tens of thousands of cranes stopped off in September-October and February-March. Though numbers vary, some tens of thousands of cranes overwinter here too. Feeding points, using maize, have helped to reduce damage to crops. But milder winters here, as in the UK, seem to have made it possible for cranes to spend the winter farther north, rather than fly to Spain. There has been a clear link between wintering birds in the Horsey area then staying to nest, so it seems reasonable to assume that if climate change does mean milder winters – albeit an uncertain assumption – then good winter survival in UK, without the hazards of migration, should be favourable for cranes in the UK.

Pinning precise numbers on these trends is tricky, but it seems fair to hazard a guess that the British Isles could have around 200 pairs of cranes in 2060 – 50 years' time from now. Even if this proves over-optimistic, there seems little doubt that more people will be enjoying the privilege of seeing cranes, from time to time if not in their daily lives, much as we have at Horsey.

Part Three
Cranes in Europe
Nick Upton

Chapter 12
Following cranes from Scandinavia to Spain

Wildlife filmmaker Dr Nick Upton spent two years close to breeding and migrating cranes in several parts of Europe. He became very familiar with the habits and characters of both the birds and their enthusiastic human guardians from Norfolk to Somerset and from Poland to Spain, which is where his story begins.

We knew the cranes were coming. Tens of thousands of them if predictions were right, but I'd learnt to be wary of forecasts where cranes were concerned; the weather might close in again or they might decide to stop somewhere on the way, for another week or so, maybe ...

Cranes over village in Gascony, France; the Pyrenees are in the background.

After three weeks of waiting in the Spanish Pyrenees, in which time we'd only seen a few straggling lines of cranes flying by in the distance between bouts of heavy snow, strong southerly winds and thick fog, time was running out for us to see and film the great migration spectacle we'd come for. We'd had false dawns before with predictions of major flights south proving false as the heaviest autumn snow for 40 years fell on the Pyrenees, and most of Europe's cranes were still feeding and resting further north. This time, though, I was more optimistic; two days earlier, while sheltering from another snow blizzard on a mountain ridge, I'd taken an excited call from Dr Martin Kraft, a dedicated German crane enthusiast, who announced "We have mass migration over Marburg!" and then held up his mobile phone. I heard the sound of a thousand crane voices as large flocks of migrants flew over him at the university and knew they were finally heading our way in big numbers, but would they really keep coming?

I've been lucky enough to work with the RSPB Film Unit over the last two years directing shoots with cameraman Toby Hough around Europe for two films about cranes, both of which feature their return to the UK. In early November 2008, we were based near the Lindux pass in the Pyrenees mountains, hoping to film one of Europe's greatest wildlife spectacles, the passage of crane flocks on their way from breeding sites across northern Europe to their wintering headquarters in central Spain and Portugal. Our shoot had begun well in early October at Lac du Der-Chantecoq in Champagne, France, to the east of Paris. Clear skies and gentle northeast winds had encouraged cranes to begin their great autumn migration south. We'd witnessed and filmed the numbers roosting on islands on the lake and feeding on agricultural fields in the area rise from around 500 to 4,000 in the week we spent there. These were just the advance guard of nearly 220,000 cranes that follow the western European flyway; they migrate southwest across Germany and France towards Spain from breeding sites across Scandinavia and Germany as well as from the Baltic States and Poland, as temperatures turn cooler in late autumn.

Some Scandinavian birds (mostly from Finland) and many more cranes from the Baltic States and Poland, along with Russian birds, take a different route south for the winter; more than 100,000 head first for the Hortobágy in Hungary, then on down to North Africa, southern Turkey and the Middle East. Cranes breeding even further east in Siberia, Mongolia and northern China winter in southern China and northern Indochina, or fly as high as airliners – at around 32,000 feet – to cross the Himalayas on their way to India.

It's believed that there are currently around 400,000 cranes living in Eurasia and the epic migrations of these large, charismatic birds attract rapt attention and seasonal celebrations in many places along their traditional routes. The journeys they undertake, though, and the numbers involved, reflect the specific needs of cranes and the history of landscape changes over time.

After centuries of decline, Eurasian crane populations have been rising steadily over the last 30 years and cranes have returned to some ancient haunts, including the UK. This resurgence is thanks to conservation efforts that have protected waterlogged breeding and roosting areas for cranes, from agricultural changes that have benefited these birds and due to the remarkable adaptability and opportunism of cranes themselves. The story is complex, though, and is also linked to the unpredictable effects of climate change. Things look good for cranes at the moment especially in western Europe, but they may need all the help they can get in the future. So understanding their needs for reproduction, feeding and what they can tolerate in terms of harsh weather and human disturbance is vital for crane conservation. Cranes towards the eastern limits of their range are believed to be in decline as many ideal habitats are under threat, though it's hard to be sure of the numbers of birds scattered across the vast wilds of Siberia, Mongolia and China. Cranes living towards the eastern end of the species' range were formerly considered to be of a separate subspecies *Grus grus lilfordi* and characteristically have paler inner secondaries, but this taxonomic distinction is no longer widely accepted. Cranes living in Northern Armenia, southern Georgia and north east Turkey do seem to differ more, however, having several plumage, egg and eye colour differences and they lack a red patch on the back of the head, and a new subspecies name of *Grus grus archibaldi* has recently been proposed for this population.

Breeding cranes traditionally prosper where there are wetlands or swampy woodlands; it's harder for ground predators such as wolves, foxes and wild boar to reach cranes nesting and roosting with water around them, as these ever alert birds hear them coming. Young chicks need lots of nutritious invertebrate food to fuel their incredible growth rates, but older chicks and adults have a broader diet, much of it vegetarian. Wild plant tubers of steppe habitats may have been an ancient staple, but today almost any agricultural crop or crop leftover provides welcome food for the adaptable crane, along with any worms, insects and even small mammals and frogs they encounter.

Cranes also do best with as little disturbance as possible. They are among the shiest and most alert birds I've ever encountered and rarely stay on the ground if approached closer than about 300 metres. They absolutely know when they're being watched (or filmed!) by anyone not in a hide and fly off if you're too close for their comfort. They'll stay on the ground, though, if you don't notice them and are looking the other way! They're clever, and seem to get used to farm vehicles and even specific people who leave them alone in areas they visit regularly. I've seen a pair of cranes in Poland, feeding on crop fields near their breeding territory, come to accept a local farmer on his tractor and his children walking to school much closer than their usual flushing distance. In Sweden and Germany, cranes accept tourists watching through telescopes or firing off volleys of camera clicks from as little as 50 to 100 yards, as long as people stay behind fixed barriers the birds have become used to. I've watched cranes stay on the ground as a tractor spread grain for them just a few feet away, but when the driver stepped out of his vehicle a hundred yards off, they all took flight. I've also seen crane nest sites within a few yards of rural roads in Poland and Germany, although they're always well hidden by dense vegetation.

A monograph on cranes written in 1881 by Edward Blyth describes how in Buddhist enclaves in Astrakhan (where living creatures would never have been threatened), cranes were said to show no fear of humans at all, but how they learnt quickly to avoid people in places where nets were set to catch them. As far as weather goes, cranes are tough birds; they seem well able to cope with very cold temperatures and their eggs are remarkably frost resistant, but they can't cope for long if food sources are hidden beneath deep snow or trapped under thick ice. Cranes really do seem to use their intelligence in reacting to new dangers, in adapting to changing weather patterns and are quick to exploit new opportunities when a new source of food appears. What cranes need and how they can adapt has influenced where they lived in the past and is now driving some recent changes to crane distribution in Europe today.

Historical records suggest that as well as being established in much of the UK, cranes once lived and bred across Europe in the Middle Ages, including countries such as Spain, Italy, Austria, and Hungary, using ancient marshlands that have now largely vanished. In former, warmer breeding areas, they may well have been non-migratory, as they would have found all they needed year round. Some populations of Eurasian cranes breeding south and east of the Black Sea in Turkey and Georgia are still believed to reside there all year or only to move short distances for the winter. This is true for the Norfolk cranes today and may have been true of UK populations in the past. As in the UK, the drainage of large areas of marsh for farming and forestry across much of Europe, combined with hunting of cranes for food, drove them from these warmer breeding areas in southern Europe. Over the centuries, their breeding range contracted hugely as they were pushed towards the northern and eastern limits of former 'crane country'; here, the less populous and harder to drain regions of Scandinavia, the Baltic States, Poland, northeast Germany and Russia still offered them quiet, wet areas for breeding, but autumn frosts triggered flights south for the winter.

Long migration routes to warmer wintering sites in Spain, Africa and the Middle East became established, with the cranes using migration stopping-off points in central Europe where they could roost in wetlands and refuel in surrounding areas. In spring, cranes migrated north again, arriving at remote breeding grounds as the last of winter snows and ice lost their grip. Cranes have become adept at timing their breeding seasons so their chicks hatch just as hordes of insects begin to emerge from wetland swamp forests, boggy pools and reedbeds around their nests, before moving their growing chicks out onto steppe, tundra or meadow habitats to forage for a mix of invertebrate and plant food. Perhaps the oldest clear record of crane migration patterns dates from 350 BC, when Aristotle described how cranes flew from the steppes of 'Scythia' (northeast of the Black Sea, an area now including the Ukraine, Kazakhstan and southern Russia) to the marshlands at the source of the Nile south of Egypt, where they were said to fight with the pygmies!

The extent of crane migration – at least along the western flyway – seems to have shrunk consistently in recent centuries, as cranes sensibly fly only as far as they really need to. Until a hundred years ago, records suggest that the majority of cranes taking the western route travelled as far as Morocco, with a few thousand staying in central Spain and Portugal. Today, that situation is reversed as few cranes now winter in Morocco and ever more do so in Iberia. This may partly reflect climate changes, but agricultural changes are likely to have influenced the birds most, as winter food supplies grew in Iberia and may have dwindled in Africa. The traditional wintering grounds for cranes in Iberia were the extensive *dehesa* landscapes of oak parkland thinned from ancient oak forests, which support a vast array of wildlife of all kinds alongside traditional, sustainable agricultural uses. This landscape has been managed in an almost unchanged way since the Middle Ages and evidence for early *dehesas* dates from the Neolithic period, over 5,000 years ago. Cranes wintering in *dehesas* feed largely on abundant acorns from holm oaks and to a lesser extent cork oaks, sometimes sharing grazing pasture beneath the trees with pigs, cattle and sheep and feeding on worms and various other plant roots, along with some wheat where this is planted under the oaks.

Cork oak *dehesa* in Extremadura.

This ancient *dehesa* farming system has been changing rapidly since the 1960s as more diverse crops, often irrigated, have proliferated, and while *dehesas* are still very important to cranes, these adaptable birds have found new food sources as well. *Dehesas* came under threat as demand for cork slumped when more and more wine producers began sealing bottles with plastic stoppers or metal screw tops. Economic pressures and EU farming policies led to many *dehesas* being used more intensively, and where they became overstocked and overgrazed, oaks failed to regenerate and the land has become more open and arid. The increased value of wheat and maize has encouraged many farmers to grub up *dehesa* oaks and to plant more of these grain crops and – bizarrely in a naturally dry region – rice paddies have also multiplied, irrigated water channelled down from mountain reservoirs. Irrigated, intensive fruit farming, with virtually no value to wildlife, has also taken off recently. All of these changes are hugely detrimental to the array of rare and special insects, reptiles, amphibians, bird and mammals that thrive in traditional *dehesas*.

For now, at least, the adaptable crane is prospering. Always a true generalist and opportunist, many cranes have switched from feeding on acorns to scavenging for leftover maize and rice. Far from populations in Spain falling, they've actually more than trebled in the last 20 years from an estimated 40,000 in 1988 to the 152,000 counted in a detailed census in 2007. The future is already bleak for the exceptional biodiversity of Spain's shrinking *dehesas* and for cranes it is also uncertain. Farming activities in Europe are increasingly driven by rapidly changing trends in crop prices and should demand for maize and rice falter, these crops might decline again. If the climate continues to warm, the supply of irrigating water could dry up and these new food sources could dwindle in Spain, even if demand for them stayed high. Once lost, a *dehesa* land-scape of mature oaks would probably never regenerate, so Spain might one day offer far less for cranes, as it already does for many other species.

Will cranes actually need to fly all the way to Spain for the winter in the future, though, as more winter food is now available further north and winter temperatures have generally increased? In the same way that maize production has grown in Spain, it has also increased hugely in Germany and France along the cranes' migration route. This has meant that cranes have a plentiful supply of food at their major stop-off points – and their migration in late autumn coincides with a wave of maize harvesting along their route. The mass of spilt grain and broken corn cobs left by the harvesters provides a feast for cranes without causing any conflict with farmers. With so much food available around major migration stop-off sites such as Lac du Der and Arjuzanx in south-west France, cranes seem to linger longer along their route every year, and more and more have begun to spend entire winters at their former temporary re-fuelling areas. This may also reflect that very cold icy, snowy winters have become rarer, though not unheard of, as the 2009/2010 winter proved. 5-13,000 cranes now winter at Lac du Der and 12-18,000 at Arjuzanx in most years and even in 2009/2010, numbers at these sites were close to 7,000 and 16,000 respectively. Other pockets of wintering cranes have appeared in France at St Martin de Seignanx near Biarritz and Lac de Puydarrieux near Tarbes where winter counts have been rising steadily. A total of around 60,000 in the Landes de Gascogne region as a whole in the winter of 2009/2010 was reported at the European Crane Conference in Germany in October 2010. Cranes have prospered as maize acreage has increased but, as in Spain, if planting policy changed or harvesting machines continue to become more efficient, there could be less easy food for cranes in the future.

Maize, though, isn't the only crop that cranes take advantage of, and when migrants descend in numbers on growing crops such as winter wheat or potatoes, conflicts with farmers can occur. Across the crane migration route from north and northeast Europe to Spain, wherever cranes threaten growing crops, varied and imaginative scaring techniques are deployed against them. These range from basic gas cannons, parked cars, striped plastic ribbons and scarecrows in fields to rotating colourful or mirrored beacons, inflatable shrieking dummies and noisy fireworks. Crafty cranes, though, are rarely put off for long and just move to the next field to resume feeding! To defuse such conflict, farmers in many countries are now compensated for foraging and trampling damage if they can prove that cranes were the culprits. Also, they've increasingly been advised to re-time planting of crops, sometimes using different varieties, to try to avoid vulnerable young crops from appearing just as the cranes do. However, with the timing of cranes' peak migration waves varying by several weeks from year to year, that's not always easy to do.

Extra corn being spread from a tractor on maize stubble. Rügen-Bock region, Germany, October 2009.

Another approach that has been working well is to lure cranes to certain crops that have been set aside for them, often with extra grain scattered daily, paid for by local government or conservation bodies. Where easy food is available at sites where they are not repeatedly chased off, cranes soon learn to take advantage. If safe roost sites are available nearby, a predictable pattern of repeated flights between roost sites and favourite feeding locations becomes established, all of which is perfect for the growing crane tourism industry around Europe (and for film crews seeking great crane footage without spending weeks waiting!).

The best known site for crane tourism in Europe is undoubtedly Lake Hornborga in southern Sweden. The story of this site shows how effective crane conservation measures can be and how quickly these intelligent birds can take advantage of new opportunities. Migrating cranes have used this wetland area, surrounded by an agricultural landscape, for at least a hundred years; traditionally cranes roosted on the lake and fed on the leftovers of potatoes grown for the vodka industry. Many Swedes welcomed and celebrated the return of cranes as a sure sign that spring was on its way. After the last distillery closed in 1971, though, crane numbers quickly declined until hundreds rather than thousands used the area on migration. The lake also became silted up, overgrown and unattractive to cranes seeking open water for roosting, but in 1995 efforts to encourage cranes back began with support from the local government. Water levels were raised in the lake and cattle were allowed to graze the margins to keep them clear; special crop fields were set aside for cranes to exploit and grain was spread daily in the southern part of the lake during spring migration periods. The cranes soon returned in numbers, more of them year on year and the peak count rose to a new record of 18,500 on 1st April 2009, with these massed migrants eating over six tons of scattered barley grain per day. Fortunately for us, we chose that year to film at the lake and secured spectacular scenes of massed cranes dancing in the snow and feeding en masse around the lake, before they headed off to their main breeding sites further north.

Despite the cost of crane conservation at Lake Hornborga, the birds are undoubtedly paying their way. More than 250,000 people visit the lake in the course of a year to see, hear and photograph cranes, generating a significant income for local conservation bodies (the barley is partly paid for by income from parking fees at viewing areas) but also for local hotels, guest houses, shops and restaurants. The cranes roost safely in the northern part of the lake, and most fly down to the main visitor centre 'Trandansen' (crane dance) on the southwest shore to gorge on the grain scattered for them, so far fewer bother to visit farmers' fields in the area. Some that do are searching for a variety of foods, including a crane favourite, worms, in pastureland rather than raiding crops. Any conflict with farmers that remains is at least softened by the wealth that the birds bring to the area and crane scientists advise farmers on how to minimise problems. As the Hornborga area has grown in popularity for migrant cranes, the number of breeding pairs has also increased year on year and some 30 pairs now breed nearby.

A similar mix of feeding sites and cranes flights to and from predictable roosts also now attracts significant crane tourism to the Rügen-Bock region of northern Germany. Great views of foraging crane flocks are guaranteed in migration periods at the Gunz and Hohendorf feeding sites and boat trips allow views of evening flights and roosts around the Werder-Bock islands. Lac du Der-Chantecoq in France is also attracting more and more crane tourists in migration periods. Spain has been slower off the mark, but crane watching has now taken off at Lake Gallocanta, a major migration stop-off point just south of the Pyrenees, and crane festivals have been established here and in Moheda Alta village in Extremadura.

Crane tourism sites across Europe also provide perfect opportunities for gathering migration information as colour-ringed birds from across the breeding range can be identified and reported. Some individuals have been sighted dozens of times in the course of several years at many sites along their migration route from northern Europe to Spain. One colour-ringed bird (blue, blue, black, yellow, red, white from the top of the left leg) that we filmed at Lac du Der, for example, has also been recorded in years before and since at its breeding site near Berlin, on migration in southern France and northern Spain and in its wintering grounds in Extremadura.

Crane tourism, when properly managed, seems to work really well for both cranes and people and the allure of cranes has proved universal. There seems to be something about their size, the haunting power of their voices, their exuberant dancing and their dedicated family nature that appeal to us humans. Wherever cranes gather in numbers, eager bands of 'craniacs' also gather, braving cold misty mornings in Sweden, France and Germany to watch the noisy spectacle of morning flights from roosts to feeding sites, and the same people gather again at dusk to see them fly back again. As a film crew, we've often been there alongside them, and I've met many expert photographers and wildlife filmmakers who describe how they strive year after year to get ever better shots of these birds flying, courting and raising their young. I'm sure it's the challenge these shy birds pose that drives them to keep trying for the perfect shots.

'Craniacs' gather to watch cranes (including those pictured on page 112) in the Rügen-Bock region of Germany, October 2009.

The appeal and intelligent adaptability of cranes was best summed up for me by Hermann Dirks, a city planner by trade, an expert wildlife photographer by hobby and a self-confessed true craniac by nature. He gave up much of his valuable spare time to guide us around the rural tracks and peat bogs on his home patch, the Diepholzer Moorniederung (Diepholzer fen lowland) of northwest Germany which has become one of Europe's most recent crane havens. Hermann told me how cranes first worked their magic on him in Sweden in 1983, at a time when he'd seen none of the few that had visited his region of Germany. While walking quietly, he'd surprised a pair of cranes on their Swedish tundra pool territory. The birds reacted by raising their bustles, lifting their heads and giving the crane's classic, defiant unison duet. He described how that haunting sound sent shivers down his spine and he was struck by the charisma and beauty of these birds. From that moment on, he was entranced by cranes and was drawn back to Sweden year after year to watch and photograph cranes. Something odd happened a few years later, though, as cranes began coming to Hermann in droves! From 1984 onwards, groups of migrant cranes occasionally began to appear in the Diepholzer Moorniederung and in the autumn of the year 2000, 20,000 cranes arrived! Violent easterly gales had blown many migrating groups off course as they headed south and they ended up in Hermann's area, well to the west of their usual route.

These cranes made the most of the situation and soon realised they'd stumbled across crane heaven: the entire region was once raised bog, much of which had been dug for peat for centuries. Many of the abandoned peat beds have been allowed to regenerate naturally, creating perfect roost sites for cranes in a complex of large boggy pools, often within protected reserve areas. Many other excavated peat beds are now farmed intensively, and have been increasingly planted with maize. The proliferation of biogas plants in the area has fuelled an ever-increasing demand for this crop, since vast amounts of maize silage and ground maize cobs are needed to fuel their fermenting tanks. Today there are always plenty of maize leftovers once the protracted autumn harvest begins ahead of migrant cranes arriving in October. Since the area is still highly prone to water-logging, heavy harvesting machines can't always get onto all the fields and some crops are left standing and available for hungry cranes throughout the winter. Opportunists that they are, more and more cranes have been coming to the Diepholzer Moorniederung in recent years, and during the autumn migration period 30-80,000 now stay around for a month or so, and 2-8,000 have usually remained all winter.

Cranes fly close to wind turbines, Lower Saxony, Germany, October 2009.

As with other modern crane havens, though, there are some new risks as well. This open, breezy region has a high density of wind farms and cranes often fly alarmingly close to the giant turbine blades as the birds shuttle between the surrounding fields. There is no clear evidence I know of that cranes actually fly into wind turbines, but Hermann and other crane conservation-ists fear that as crane and turbine numbers rise, major accidents are sure to happen on foggy days, when flocks feeding close to a wind farm might be disturbed and take off in a panic. What is certain is that the huge pylon lines that march across the countryside are already a threat, as cranes often skim just over them while flying to and from their roost sites, and more pylons are planned for the area. We came across and filmed a dead crane with a recently broken wing directly under a big pylon line on a foggy November morning in 2009, and wires sometimes take out many birds at once. I was told by Patrick Dulau of the Arjuzanx reserve in southwest France, the biggest overwintering site for cranes north of the Pyrenees, that nearly a hundred cranes were killed by some low overhead wires in one very foggy day in his area. Wires clearly can take an important toll on cranes and high fences in Spain are also known to be lethal for these birds. Hermann also believes that uncontrolled crane tourism is a growing danger to cranes in the Diepholzer Moorniederung. At Rehdener Geestmoor, there is a wonderful multi-level tower hide for watching cranes fly in to roost on the peat moors it overlooks, but Hermann has seen the proliferation of cars and crane watchers on the road that bisects the moor cause disturbance and confusion for late-arriving cranes. As Hermann also described, we often saw crane enthusiasts using a maze of agricultural back roads to search for feeding flocks by day and they often flushed cranes from fields close to pylon lines by getting out of their cars. Access may need to become more restricted, as it now is in the Rügen-Bock area of Germany where roads through some crane feeding zones are closed except to farmers during crane migration periods.

Crane flock flying just over electricity cables strung between pylons on their way to a night-time roost. Lower Saxony, Germany, autumn 2009.

The Diepholzer Moorniederung story shows how well cranes can adapt to a changing Europe, but also hints at some inherent dangers of modern landscapes. It also shows how what had become viewed as traditional migration routes can change if the cranes find new places they like. Cranes also began to breed in the Diepholzer Moorniederung in 2004 and numbers nesting across Lower Saxony have risen to nearly 500 pairs. This follows a general pattern of cranes re-establishing themselves over a wider geographic range in recent decades after retreating to the margins of their former range centuries ago. The Diepholzer Moorniederung is not far from the Netherlands, and cranes may well spread across the border. As the Norfolk story shows, a few cranes blown further west than usual on migration are quite capable of establishing new breed-ing sites if they find all that they need.

One that didn't make it: a broken wing caused by flying into a cable. Lower Saxony, Germany, autumn 2009.

The growing success story of cranes at the Diepholzer Moorniederung and elsewhere in Europe provides some parallels with their return to the UK, and offers some warnings as well. Norfolk cranes were well served by the protective isolation offered on the Horsey estate and the general inaccessibility of much of the Broadland landscape to people. The same should be true for those released on the Somerset Levels and Moors by the Great Crane Project from autumn 2010 onwards, but thought will need to be put into how to manage crane tourism. It's important that feeding birds and most especially breeding birds will not be disturbed by well meaning visitors or become targeted by the surviving breed of obsessive, illegal egg collectors. Predators are also always likely to take a toll of crane eggs and chicks as they do in Europe. I was told that up to 50% of nests fail in parts of Poland due to the attentions of ravens, crows and wild boar especially. In the UK, corvids and foxes are a likely threat, but cranes have always coped with natural threats and, given the right environment and enough protection from human threats, I'd expect British crane populations to grow in the west, once established, as well as in the Norfolk-originated eastern population.

Personally, I've had some great experiences watching and photographing cranes. As with Hermann Dirk's experience in Sweden, I was enthralled by cranes ever since my first encounter with them in Spain fifteen years ago: large, noisy flocks put on quite a show for me as they flew past an ancient hilltop castle on a spectacularly red sky evening, before gathering at their roost site in a mountain reservoir beneath my look-out point. I'll never forget recording crane calls reverberating around the alder swamps of Biebrza marshes in Poland, as the territorial trumpeting of numerous pairs carried to me from miles away in all directions. I treasure the moment when I saw flocks of migrating cranes coming in off the Baltic Sea from Sweden, to reach Germany's northernmost point at Cape Arkona, on a stormy day in October. Seeing my first British cranes at Horsey with John Buxton as my guide was also a big thrill and a great privilege. I thought I knew Norfolk and what it has to offer well but, thanks to the care and sense with which John suppressed the news of cranes returning to Horsey, I was blithely unaware that these wonderful birds were breeding in Norfolk again until long after they'd begun to and hadn't actually seen one in the UK until 2009!

Of all my experiences with cranes, though, the most lasting one – to date anyway – came on 4th November 2008. We were in the Pyrenees after three weeks of mostly frustrated anticipation. By 3rd November, the weather was still foul up at Roncesvalles where we were staying, but the forecast for the 4th was good, and a network of crane contacts had been posting news on the internet that cranes were flooding south and that many had reached southern France. All the signs pointed to a major migration over the Pyrenees in the next 24 hours, but the weather was then due to close in again. We'd only get one chance to film what we wanted and we needed to make the most of it!

That night I began to dream that I could hear cranes flying overhead, or at least I thought I was dreaming until I got up at around 3am, opened a window to listen and realised that a few cranes were already flying over in darkness. Now I was worried again: would they all pass before the sun rose, or would the heavy snow we'd had in the last few days stop us from reaching our best viewpoints high above Lindux pass?

Before first light, cameraman Toby Hough and I drove to the ridge at the head of the Lindux valley and set up our cameras and microphones. We scanned the sky for cranes and checked the wind direction, which could affect where most flocks might pass and where we might need to move to. We'd been told that on migration days most cranes cross the Pyrenees between mid morning and mid afternoon, but that on peak days they often start flying earlier and continue migrating into the night. Before long we saw the first group of the day, flapping hard to gain altitude as they worked their way up the valley and passed over a ridge of trees to our left. We got a few shots, but knew we needed to get higher to have a wider view and to see in as many directions as possible.

We knew that the side roads to the higher viewpoints would be tricky to get up. Snow ploughs had only cleared the main through routes and we'd twice got our Land Rover stuck in frozen snow drifts trying to reach the best viewpoints in the last two days, but today we really had to get as high as possible. As we headed up a track to the west of the pass, we realised that although the snow was a bit softer, our favourite outlook on a high ridge above the valley directly on the France /Spain border would be impossible to reach. Instead, we decided to get as close as we could to the remains of Lindux fort, where a team of French ornithologists from the Organbidexka Col Libre migration monitoring team were counting all kinds of bird over a two month period. Snow and thick mist had confined them to their tents in the woods nearby by for the last three days and we knew they were hoping for a good, clear day as much as us. With our Land Rover's gears set in low ratio, we made it most of the way up to the fort, passing ranks of hunters' blinds and towers, many of them filling up in anticipation of a major pigeon passage that day, and parked alongside some hunters' vehicles with Lindux fort ahead of us. That left us just a few hundred steep yards to climb up to the mountain-top escarpments of the fort through deep snow, carrying our film camera, lenses, tripod, sound equipment, my stills camera and lots of food and hot drinks for the day ahead.

Cranes approach the French Pyrenees, December 2009.

It was certainly a long day, but also a real 'red letter' one. By the end of it we'd seen around 20,000 cranes, lit by bright sunshine, passing by us in flocks of between 15 and 800, with snowy mountains and ridges all around. None passed very near, but many were close enough to get the classic migration scenes we'd hoped for as large flocks flew by us with a spectacular wintry mountainscape behind them, and some huge multi-V flocks passed directly over us. As we'd been told would happen, they flew quite low in the morning, often barely skimming the trees and ridges with their wings beating hard much of the time. By late morning, as thermals began to give them some lift, they began to circle above the lower peaks and gained tremendous height before moving on south with occasional flaps and long glides. At times we could see seven or eight flocks at once and Julien Traversier and his OCL team could barely keep up with their counting work. Using powerful telescopes, they were seeing flocks long before we did, up to four miles away, but even at that range we could actually hear the biggest flocks coming. Toby shot a lot of film that day and I kept busy scanning for flocks, recording sound, taking photographs and made two more trips back to the Land Rover to fetch more film, a video camera to use as light levels dipped and to get more chocolate! After such a long wait, it was a huge relief to know we'd achieved what we'd come for. Julien did some quick sums and told us that he'd compiled the second highest daily crane count ever recorded from one site in the Pyrenees, almost matching 22,000 seen in November 2004, again after a long period of poor weather. We knew we'd witnessed something pretty special and it did prove to be our only chance; many more cranes flew over in darkness that night and just a few more in foggy, unfilmable conditions the next day. It was time for us to move on.

Cranes over the high Pyrenees, November 2008.

Nearly eighteen months on, I've seen a lot more cranes in many different places, and I still feel privileged each time I see them again. The return of cranes to the UK from the continent of Europe after a 400 year absence, which began in Norfolk with John Buxton's invaluable help, is a story with many more chapters to be written. It's a story that I believe will come to affect a lot of people across the UK, as these spectacular and engaging birds re-establish and reassert themselves in their traditional haunts, and I feel very fortunate to have the chance to tell some of it.

The RSPB Film Unit's 'Crane Country' is about the return to the UK of both wild and captive reared cranes. The film includes an interview with John Buxton and has some of his historic archive film footage, shot between 1979 and 1989, of the first cranes to breed in the UK for 400 years. It can be viewed on the Great Crane Project website www.thegreatcraneproject.org.uk

References and further reading

Boisseau, S., and Yalden, D. W. 1998. The former status of the Crane *Grus grus* in Britain. *Ibis,* 140: 482-500.
Cocker, Mark and Mabey, Richard. 2005. *Birds Britannica.* Chatto & Windus, London.
Cramp, S & Simmons, KEL, 1980. *The Birds of the Western Palearctic,* Volume II. OUP.
D'Arcy, Gordon. 1993. *Ireland's Lost Birds.* Four Courts Press, Dublin.
Ellis, E.A. 1965. *The Broads.* Collins, London.
Gantlett, Steve. 1991. The Cranes of Broadland. *Birding World* 4(2): 66-68
George, Martin. 1992. *The land use, ecology and conservation of Broadland.* Packard Publishing, Chichester.
Holloway, Simon. 1996. *The Historical Atlas of Breeding Birds in Britain and Ireland.* T & A D Poyser (p.433).
Klosowscy, Grzegorz and Tomasz. 2000. *Crane, the Bird of Hope.* Fundacja Ochrony Zasobow Naturalnych RP 'Ekopol', Warsaw.
Lundin, Goran. 2005. *Cranes, where, when and why.* Swedish Ornithological society, Morbylanga.
Moreau, Gaston. 1990. Une nouvelle espèce nidificatrice pour la France: la Grue cendrée Grus grus. *Alauda* 58 (4), 1990.
Moss, Brian. 2001. *The Broads.* New Naturalist, HarperCollins, London.
Nowald, Günter and Donner, Norman (Editors). 2010. *Conference programme and abstract volume of the VIIth European crane Conference.*
Taylor, Moss; Seago, Michael; Allard, Peter and Don Dorling. 1999. *The Birds of Norfolk.* Pica Press, Norfolk (pp. 229-231)
Newbery, P (RSPB), Jarrett, N (Wildfowl and Wetlands Trust), Jordan, D (Pensthorpe Conservation Trust), Andrew Reeve, A (PCT), Mark Trinder, M (WWT) and Fouracre, D (RSPB). 2006. *Crane translocation project feasibility study.*
Norfolk and Norwich Naturalists' Society, 2008 and earlier. *Norfolk Bird and Mammal Reports* (various dates).
Sills, Norman. 2007. *Lakenheath Fen Cranes 2007.* Unpublished confidential RSPB report.
Sills, Norman. 2008. The Return of Nesting Cranes *Grus grus* to the Fens of eastern England.
Sills, Norman. 2017. *The Cranes of Lakenheath Fen.* British Wildlife, June 2017.
Stanbury, Andrew and Sills, Norman. 2012. *Common Crane habitats in Britain.* British Wildlife, August 2012.
Stanbury, Andrew and the UK Crane Working Group. 2011. *The Changing Status of Common Cranes in the UK.* British Birds, August 2011.
Suffolk Birds 2007. The Suffolk Naturalists' Society 2008.
Stevenson, Henry. 1870. *The Birds of Norfolk.* Vol. 2. John van Doorst and Gurney & Jackson, London.

Unpublished crane reports from Horsey

Anderson, Sandra. 1983. *The Grey Crane Grus grus at Horsey.* Unpublished report. Buxton, J J. 1993. *Observations of the behaviour of European cranes Grus grus in relation to the breeding season in east Norfolk 1979 to 1992.* Unpublished notes.
Buxton, J J. 1995. *The European Crane in the United Kingdom of Great Britain in 1985.* Paper presented at International crane Foundation Working Group on European cranes, 21–26 October 1985, Orozháza–Kardoshút, Hungary.
Scott, Hilary. 1983. *Common Cranes Grus grus in Britain.* Unpublished notes.
Leaper, Genevieve. 1986. *The Common Crane.* 1986 breeding season at Horsey. Unpublished report.
MacDonald, Minette. 1985. *Untitled.* Unpublished crane wardening report.

Useful websites

Horsey Village **www.horseyvillage.com**
Norfolk Wildlife Trust **www.norfolkwildlifetrust.org.uk**
Pensthorpe Conservation Trust **www.pensthorpetrust.org.uk**
RSPB **www.rspb.org.uk**
The Great Crane Project **www.thegreatcraneproject.org.uk**
The National Trust **www.nationaltrust.org.uk**
The Norfolk Cranes' Story **www.norfolkcranes.co.uk**
Wildfowl & Wetlands Trust **www.wwt.org.uk**

European crane websites

Count data from the main crane sites on **www.grus-grus.eu**
Crane Information Centre (mostly in German) **www.kraniche.de**
iCORA: an online database for recoveries of colour-ringed and radio-tagged Eurasian Cranes **www.icora.de**

The Great Crane Project is a partnership project between the Wildfowl & Wetlands Trust, the RSPB, Pensthorpe Conservation Trust and Viridor Credits.

Appendices

Appendix 1 – Guide to crane pairs A to E

Pair A. The first pair that appeared in the autumn of 1979 and first attempted to nest in 1981. Called the 'number one pair' in the Horsey Estate notebooks. They nested for nine years in a row, the last year being 1989, before disappearing in the winter of 1989-90. They successfully produced young in 1982 (a male), 1983 (a female) and 1986 (a female).

Pair B. The young produced by Pair A in 1982 and 1983, a sibling pair. In the Horsey notebooks in the later years these are often (and confusingly!) called the 'number 1 pair', after the original pair disappeared. They first nested at Horsey in 1988, producing a chick that year. Their second offspring was the imprinted bird, still at Pensthorpe. They then had a run of unsuccessful years before possibly fledging two young in 1997 (the juveniles that were first seen in December of that year), then two again in 1999, one in 2003 and one in 2005. It is probably this pair that continues to nest in the Fen up to the present, fledging one young in 2008, two in 2009 and one in 2010. If these suppositions are correct, they have fledged at least nine cranes, or 11 if they did fledge two in 1997, and so have played a key role in the cranes' re-colonisation of the UK.

Pair C. A bird that arrived in autumn 1985 as a young bird of that year, but not, apparently, home-bred; plus the young reared by Pair A in 1986. Infertile, perhaps due to lead shot found in the male bird in a post-mortem after it died in 2002. First nested in 1991.

Pair D. These became established as a fourth pair in 1991 but did not nest successfully until 1997. The origin of these is not certain, but it is quite likely that they were a young male produced in 1988, paired with a migrant female arriving in 1989. It was this pair that first successful fledged chicks away from Horsey in 2001 in another river valley. They remain in the winter flock in the Horsey-Hickling area.

Pair E. This pair started to nest regularly in 1998, then just outside the Horsey Estate, a pattern that continued most years thereafter. Their origin is not completely certain, but the male of the pair is thought to be the first chick fledged by Pair B in 1988 with a female migrant arriving in 1991 as a young bird. Both birds of Pair E have grey bustles so are easy to distinguish from Pair D, both of which have black bustles.

Appendix 2 – Cranes year by year in Horsey and Broadland[1]

Winter	Maximum number[2]	Year	Nesting pairs, Horsey[3]	Fledging success	Nesting pairs, Broadland[4]	Comments
1979/80	4	1980	-	-	-	Young pair present, did not nest
1980/81	2	1981	1	0	-	-
1981/82	2	1982	1	1 (male)	-	-
1982/83	4	1983	1	1 (female)	-	-
1983/84	4	1984	1	0	-	-
1984/85	4	1985	1	0	-	-
1985/86	5	1986	1	1	-	-
1986/87	6	1987	1	0	-	-
1987/88	6	1988	2	1	-	-
1988/89	9	1989	2	0	-	-
1989/90	8	1990	1	0	-	-
1990/91	6	1991	2	0	-	-
1991/92	6	1992	3	0	-	One young raised at Pensthorpe from an egg taken under licence
1992/93	8	1993	3	0	-	-
1993/94	9	1994	3	0	-	-
1994/95	6	1995	3	0	-	-
1995/96	16+	1996	2[5]	0	-	-
1996/97	12	1997	3	2 (4?)	-	See 1997 account for fledging success
1997/98	10	1998	4	1	-	-
1998/99	11	1999	4	2	-	-
1999/00	13	2000	4	0	-	-

Winter	Maximum number[2]	Year	Nesting pairs, Horsey[3]	Fledging success	Nesting pairs, Broadland[4]	Comments
2000/01	11	2001	3	1	4	First year with a nest away from Horsey which fledged 2
2001/02	16	2002	3	0	4	-
2002/03	15	2003	2	1-2	4	First nest at Hickling
2003/04	28	2004	2	0	4	Winter max on 2nd Jan 2004
2004/05	34	2005	3	3	5	Winter max of 34 included at least 5 juveniles
2005/06	36	2006	2	0	5	Winter flock included a juvenile thought to be from Yorkshire
2006/07	33	2007	3	1	7	The nest was adjacent but one chick fledged at Horsey
2007/08	40+	2008	2	3	8-9	A third pair did not nest
2008/09	50	2009	3	3	10	Flock of 46 plus family of 4
2009/10	51	2010	3	1	8-9	-
2010/11	44	2011	2-3	0	5	-
2011/12	50	2012	2-3	4	6	-
2012/13	63	2013	2-4	1-3	5	-

1. Some information in this table may be incomplete. The UK Crane Working Group is working on a definitive history of cranes in the UK since re-colonisation, which is likely to fine-tune some figures.
2. Winter maxima are either from Horsey records or the Norfolk Bird Report (NBR). In the early years, these usually match, but the higher figure is used when they do not. Examples include 1993/94 when the NBR records a maximum eight wintering cranes in 1993/94, but there is a record of nine in the Horsey notebooks, and 2003/4. Peak counts, especially in later years, are often from outside the Horsey Estate.
3. Only pairs known to attempt to nest are included in the Horsey and Broadland totals. Two birds summering together without being known to nest are excluded from these figures. Included within these Horsey totals are nests just off the estate to the south, these birds always bringing their chicks to feed at Horsey so were effectively fledged from Horsey.
4. Until 2001, all nesting attempts were at Horsey or immediately adjacent to Horsey.
5. This drop to two pairs is surprising: there is the possibility of an additional pair with details in a notebook that could be missing.

Away from the Broads, there was one pair in Yorkshire from 2002 and two pairs at Lakenheath Fen from 2007. Information on these and other cranes in the UK is collated by the UK Crane Working Group.

Appendix 3 – UK Crane Working Group

The UK Crane Working Group is the official umbrella organisation for conservation bodies, land managers and other private individuals concerned with crane conservation in the UK.

The main aims and work of the Group are to:

- Protect sites used by cranes for breeding and roosting.

- Undertake conservation management to benefit and encourage cranes.

- Monitor and record breeding attempts and the population as a whole.

- Monitor and record population spread away from the core areas.

- Monitor and record crane sightings elsewhere in the UK.

- Maintain a database on UK crane information and data.

- Provide advice to land owners and land managers on crane habitat requirements.

- Produce an Action Plan for UK crane conservation.

- Maintain links with other Crane Working Groups in Europe.

- Promote the work of the UK Crane Working Group and UK cranes in general.

Some partners also:

Through cranes, provide information and inspiration to engage people in the conservation of cranes and the wetlands on which they depend.

The Group would be interested to receive sightings of cranes away from the core areas and particularly records during the breeding season. All records are treated in confidence. Contact email: ukcwg@yahoo.co.uk

The picture is a scan of prints joined together, then converted to black and white; the original colour digital images were lost. Seventeen of a flock of 22 cranes at Waxham, October 2009. Five of the flock were juveniles.

Appendix 4 – John Buxton, obituary

This obituary was published in the journal British Birds in May 2014. The story of the cranes is closely linked to John's involvement with them, so it seems fitting to include this for the information about John and as a tribute to him and his work. The obituary was written in 'BB' house style with capital letters plus scientific names for wildlife species and these are kept here. This is slightly longer than the published version which was reduced to fit the available space.

John Joseph Buxton (1927–2014)

John Buxton, who died at his home – Horsey Hall, Norfolk – on 11th January 2014, was the central character in the protection of Common Cranes *Grus grus* on their return as a British breeding bird. He was the Cranes' guardian for more than three decades, was an accomplished wildlife film-maker and made a great contribution to protecting wildlife in his corner of the Broads. Conservation runs in the Buxton family. In 1903, John's grandfather Edward North Buxton was a founder member of Fauna and Flora International (formerly the Fauna and Flora Preservation Society).

John was born in Geneva in 1927 as his father, Anthony, worked there for the League of Nations. Disenchanted, Major Anthony Buxton left Switzerland and bought the Horsey Estate in 1930. John's first memory of Horsey was as a four-year-old where, he later recalled, the water and the reedbeds always fascinated him. His father's commitment to protecting the Horsey Estate led him to pass the freehold to the National Trust. The arrangement for the Buxton family to manage the estate on a 99-year lease continues today.

As a child, John saw damage to the Horsey area when the sea broke through in 1938, when the impact was worse than in the floods of 1953. After three years with the army in post-war Germany, he was trained in agricultural management, spending time on a relative's farm in Suffolk and in Canada. Taking over the estate's management in 1958, it became his life's work to manage and protect the area's freshwater marshes. Marsh Harriers *Circus aeruginosus* and Eurasian Bitterns *Botaurus stellaris* returned to breed.

John made films for Anglia's Survival series after he was asked – at three days' notice – by Aubrey, later Lord Buxton, to fly to Uganda to make a programme about White Rhinos *Ceratotherium simum.* Further overseas projects followed. In 1965 John made two wildlife documentaries for the RSPB about the Norfolk broads: 'Broadland Winter' and 'Broadland Summer'. Later he filmed 'his' Cranes, and this wonderful archive footage features in recent Crane films.

In September 1979, a local farmer phoned John to report 'the biggest bloody herons I have seen in my life.' John suspected they might be Cranes, as they had moved through the area before, and so it proved. This time they stayed, albeit leaving for short periods. The first nesting attempt was in 1981, when one chick hatched but was lost to an unknown predator. They nested again in 1982 and this time fledged one young – the first Crane to be fledged in the UK for some 400 years.

The Cranes arrived as immature birds and Horsey's coastal location, mix of reed and sedge beds, grazing marsh and arable played a part in attracting the birds and tempting them to stay and nest. Another crucial factor was that Horsey was remarkably free from disturbance by people. This, and the fear of egg-collectors, meant John was zealous in maintaining privacy for the Cranes' first decade there. Many birdwatchers will recall being firmly steered away. Glen Tyler, carrying out Bittern research, was one of these, when John caught him canoeing along a ditch at about 04:30. Yet I've never met anyone who holds a grudge on account of being asked to leave, based as it was on a passion to protect Cranes. Indeed, John was the perfect gentleman to anyone who got to know him.

Crane protection in the early years was shared between John, wardens from the Horsey Estate and, for ten years, a seasonal warden employed by the RSPB. The wardens mostly stayed at Horsey Hall: John's wife Bridget shared his enthusiasm, and her hospitality was vital for many who visited or stayed.

RSPB involvement was at arm's length, which suited both the Society and John. He had a slightly ambivalent view of the RSPB: quick to make friends with individual staff members, including me, but a little suspicious of the Society's size and influence. John was relieved that that the Great Crane Project reintroducing captive-bred Cranes was in Somerset, well away from his own great Crane project in Norfolk, but he quite understood how Sir Peter Scott's Wildfowl & Wetlands Trust should be enthusiastic to see Cranes return. One of John favourite mementos was a sketch of the 'Grey birds' made when Sir Peter, with Lady Phillipa Scott, came to see the Horsey Cranes in 1985.

Secrecy was top priority in the early years of the Cranes at Horsey, though in reality these large and noisy birds were never the best kept secret. Rumours that one or more had escaped from collections helped to reduce birdwatcher interest, rumours that John did not discourage. In hindsight, it is clear that the Norfolk re-colonisation was part of a westward spread into areas from which they'd been lost in historical times. Cranes bred away from Horsey for the first time in 2001, then at nearby Hickling in 2003 and in Yorkshire and at RSPB Lakenheath Fen soon after. This encouraged John to be relaxed about publicity and he became keen to tell their story.

Sometimes ramshackle hides overlooking nesting areas were a great asset for protecting and observing the Cranes. John kept notebooks and the detailed, contemporary accounts of the Cranes' activities and behaviour were invaluable when he and I wrote *The Norfolk Cranes' Story,* first published in 2011.

John was a deputy lieutenant of Norfolk and was made an MBE for services to conservation in 2007. John and Bridget remained great travellers, visiting Scotland annually and Norway regularly. His enthusiasm for wildlife never dimmed: he would twinkle like a schoolboy naturalist when talking about the progress of some captive Swallowtail *Papilio machaon* larvae.

Countless people have fond memories as guests of John and Bridget to see Cranes, to look over the private 'scrape' at Horsey or see Pink-footed Geese *Anser brachyrhynchus* fly to roost. This affection was evident when some 500 people, including a large and loving family, gathered at Winterton-on-Sea church to celebrate his life.

Chris Durdin